San Francisco Heroes I Have Known

John A. Kerner, M.D.

iBooks

Habent Sua Fata Libelli

iBooks
Manhanset House
Dering Harbor, New York 11965-0342
Tel: 212-427-7139
bricktower@aol.com • www.ibooksinc.com

Library of Congress Cataloging-in-Publication Data

Kerner, John.
San Francisco Heroes I have Known
p. cm.

1. Biography. 2. History—San Francisco. 3. Women's
Health. 4. World War II
Nonfiction, I. Title.

ISBN-13: 978-1-59687-013-0, Trade Paper

Cover design by Ryan Kerner
Copyright © 2015 by John Kerner, M.D.

January 2015

San Francisco Heroes
I Have Known

John A. Kerner, M.D.

DEDICATION

For Gwen, a special hero for me for sixty-nine years.

Contents

Congressional Record

United States of America

PROCEEDINGS AND DEBATES OF THE 113th CONGRESS, SECOND SESSION

Vol. 160   WASHINGTON, WEDNESDAY, MARCH 5, 2014   No. 37

Senate

TRIBUTE TO DR. JOHN KERNER

Mrs. BOXER. Mr. President, I ask my colleagues to join me in celebrating the 95th birthday of Dr. John Kerner, an American hero, healthcare pioneer, and cherished doctor to so many families, including my own.

John Kerner was born in Portland, OR, and raised in Boston and San Francisco. He graduated from the University of California, Berkeley and UCSF Medical School, serving in the ROTC while in school. In 1943, he was called to active duty and commissioned as a first lieutenant.

As a battalion surgeon and combat medic in World War II, Dr. Kerner served with great distinction on the battlefields of Omaha Beach, Saint-Lô, and Bastogne. Shortly after landing in Normandy, he delivered a breech baby at a combat aid station, saving the mother and her child. On another occasion, when a group of U.S. soldiers was nearly surrounded by German SS troops, Dr. Kerner and one of his medics drove straight through the lines to deliver medical supplies and care to the wounded.

For his valiant service in World War II, Dr. Kerner was awarded the Combat Medic Badge, two Bronze Stars, five Battle Stars, and a Presidential Unit Citation. In 2007, he was awarded the Legion of Honor by French President Nicolas Sarkozy. He later recounted his experiences in a stirring memoir, "A Combat Medic Comes Home."

After the war, Dr. Kerner returned home to California, where he served the women and families of the San Francisco Bay area as an outstanding OB/GYN and the medical community as a teacher and administrator. During his residency studies at UC San Francisco, he worked closely with Dr. Herbert F. Traut, who had helped to develop the Pap smear. Along with Traut, Kerner was instrumental in ensuring that women in the community had access to these critical screenings, which drastically reduced the instances of cervical cancer. To honor Dr. Kerner and his groundbreaking work, UC San Francisco established the John A. Kerner Distinguished Professorship in Gynecologic Oncology focusing on cancer research and patient care for women.

Dr. Kerner later became the founding director of the OB/GYN Department at Mt. Zion Hospital, where he taught the next generation of physicians and served as chief of staff before establishing his own private practice. My children are among the more than 2,000 babies that he delivered over the course of his career.

Dr. John Kerner has enriched the lives of so many, from the wounded of World War II who made it home thanks to his exceptional care and courage, to the women whose health he protected and whose babies he brought into the world, to the many doctors who now do the same because he taught them how. I am honored to salute him today in the Senate.

Foreword

In a long life like mine, you have the good fortune to meet all kinds of people whom you would classify as heroes. I began to think about real heroism when I was in charge of a group of combat medics in Normandy in World War II.

Our job was to pick up wounded where they fell. We would then apply first-aid then try to get the wounded to a safe area. I had a command jeep. My driver was much older than the average G.I. He had been a driver for rumrunners in New Jersey. He not only was the best driver I had ever seen but he took loving care of our jeep's motor. We all called him "Gangster."

Our division, the 35th, was assigned to the First Army for the Normandy invasion on Omaha beach. When it was time to break out of Normandy, we were assigned to Patton's Army, the Third. On our first days during the attack all kinds of things went wrong. The worst was when our bombers bombed the front lines of one of our divisions. The other, a battalion of another division was surrounded by one of two German SS divisions sent to stop our breakout.

The surrounded battalion radioed for help. At first there was little help available. They had many wounded and no remaining medical supplies. Attempts to drop supplies failed and the Germans picked up most of them. Gangster came to me and said that he thought he could get through the German lines with medical supplies. I told him that the German SS would not respect our red crosses as he knew from the bullet holes in our jeep which had a red cross flag and red cross marks on its sides. He said it would be worth a try. He showed me the route he hoped to take and I agreed and thought I better go along because the surrounded battalion had lost its surgeons. We both agreed not to tell anyone, because higher command would have thought the whole thing crazy.

We loaded the jeep with all the available medical material we could put in it. At first daylight, we took off. Gangster revved up his carefully prepared engine and we took off over the country road that could get us to the surrounded battalion. I did not realize how fast a jeep could go. We went directly through the German lines. At first they must have thought we were one of theirs. They began to shoot at us, but by then we were just about over our U.S. lines and found shelter. Gangster never slowed no matter what bumps we had to go over. A terrible sight greeted us. The defense line surrounded what had been some sort of stone mine about a hundred yards in diameter. In that area were crowded a very large number of wounded. It reminded me of something from the Civil

War. We worked all day and through the night until we ran out of supplies, which included a fairly large number of bottles of plasma, various kinds of bandages and splints and most important morphine and cigarettes. Finally, I fell asleep, but when I awoke Gangster had not stopped. Late the next day our division broke the German line and all available ambulances were put to work. We returned to join our outfit on the rush across France. The wounded were so grateful especially for the morphine and cigarettes. No officer thanked or complimented us.

To me Gangster was a hero, and later I was able to get him a Bronze Star. I thought he deserved much more.

Of course, not all heroes are military, as I have learned, and I resolved to bring some to mind.

George Kleinsteiber "Gangster" Napleon's Chateau.
My jeep.

1   DIANNE FEINSTEIN

San Francisco was falling apart. In November 1978, an ex-supervisor, Dan White, had killed both the popular mayor George Moscone and a popular supervisor Harvey Milk. Dianne Feinstein was first on the scene. She tried to find a way to save Moscone. He quickly died in her arms. Blood stained, she realized as senior supervisor it was up to her to take control. She did. She was a hero and continues to be.

San Francisco had been dangerously divided. There had been a recent election for mayor. Moscone was popular with the working class. The gay community liked him as a defender of their group. The Unions supported him as a man of the people. Against him was Barbagelata who represented the business class especially the real estate group. The election was very close. Barbagelata was able to mount a recall vote that had failed. He continued to try to block Moscone. The police department hated Moscone who had appointed a mild, pleasant man to be chief. A group that despised the gays populated the group. Among them was a young man named Dan White who had been a fireman and policeman. White was encouraged to run for supervisor which he did and won, but once elected he found he would be earning much less than he did as a policeman. He resigned. His friends on the police force tried to get him to return as their representative. Moscone had already replaced him with a more sympathetic man. White, upset by all this, loaded his police revolver with softheaded bullets (to do more damage). He crawled through a basement window of City Hall to avoid detection of the gun. He shot the mayor five times and Harvey Milk five times. He escaped easily. Dianne Feinstein heard the shots. Her office was close by. She was first on this ghastly scene. She held Moscone in her arms while he quickly bled to death.

She pulled herself together with difficulty (Howard N. said that he held her in his arms to help control her shaking.) And from the top of the stairs in City Hall, still stained with Moscone's blood, she spoke to the gathering crowd. She said that the pain they all felt could be overcome and the city they all loved would be put back to together if she had anything to say about it. She also stated that she would continue the work of George Moscone particularly in human rights and understanding. She said bullets would not stop their progress. She was given a huge ovation certainly beyond anything she had experienced.

Two days later, she had a chance to adjust and spoke again. There was a stage draped in black on the steps of City Hall.

"Neither of the two men we mourn today was bitter or vengeful. Their deaths should not engender feelings alien to their nature or to the nature of this beautiful city. If there has been rancor between our different races and between our different lifestyles let us put it aside. Let us join together in a spirit of unity and reconciliation. Let us take pride in the memory of George Moscone and Harvey Milk and the San Francisco we love."

In organizations like cities, states, and countries it often happens when situations get bad, someone comes to the top who leads us to civic health. Dianne was the right person and again a hero in 1978. The city of San Francisco was a mess. She led in so many ways.

OFFICE OF THE MAYOR
SAN FRANCISCO

DIANNE FEINSTEIN

September 17, 1985

Dr. John Kerner
101 Spruce Street
San Francisco, CA 94118

Dear John:

How touched I was by your letter and how much pleasure I take in your words about my father!

You can pay me no greater compliment. Thank you so very much.

Warmest personal regards.

Cordially,

People said she was the only grownup in the room. She was now the mayor. She was a hero!

She got there by an unusual route. I knew her father who was the best general surgeon I had ever known. He was highly respected at the University of California Medical School in San Francisco and a full professor there. Dianne loved him dearly. Her mother was a beautiful woman, a daughter of a refugee general from Russia. Unfortunately, she had problems which some related to her having had encephalitis as a child. She had rages from time to time and Dianne was often the prime object. She frequently had to defend her two younger sisters. Dianne has said that she learned leadership at home managing her mother and her sisters. Dianne found time to study and did well in a Catholic school, Sacred Heart, from which she was accepted at Stanford. She had been raised as a Jew, though I do not think her family was especially

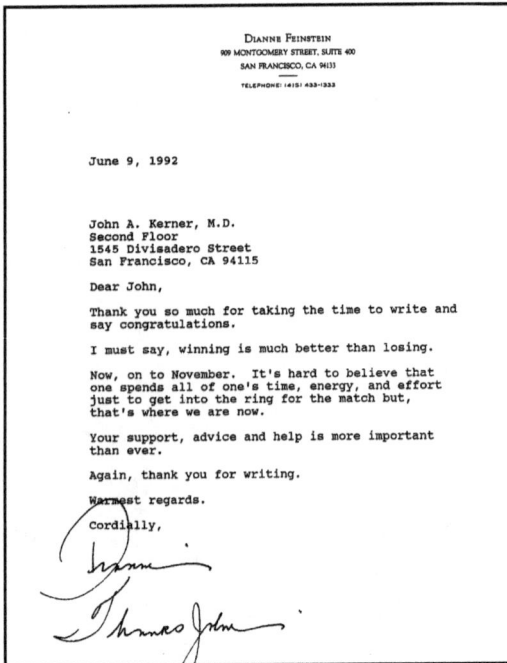

DIANNE FEINSTEIN
909 MONTGOMERY STREET, SUITE 400
SAN FRANCISCO, CA 94133

TELEPHONE: (415) 433-1333

June 9, 1992

John A. Kerner, M.D.
Second Floor
1545 Divisadero Street
San Francisco, CA 94115

Dear John,

Thank you so much for taking the time to write and say congratulations.

I must say, winning is much better than losing.

Now, on to November. It's hard to believe that one spends all of one's time, energy, and effort just to get into the ring for the match but, that's where we are now.

Your support, advice and help is more important than ever.

Again, thank you for writing.

Warmest regards.

Cordially,

Dianne

Thanks John

religious. On the other hand, Dianne has said that though she had four years in a Catholic school, she was never tempted to convert.

She did well at Stanford and was accepted to a Coro fellowship that was endowed to train students in political leadership. Fortunately, her uncle Morris was a successful coat manufacturer who loved Democratic politics. Incidentally, he told me that he had financed Leon and his brother through medical school. He took Dianne to a meeting of the Board of Supervisors not only to show her how it worked, but also to show her his influence.

She entered San Francisco politics feeling that the city needed clean, good government. She won her first try for Supervisor in 1969 as a moderate Democrat without the help of the local machine but with help from Uncle Morris. Now at 36 she was the mother of a 12-year-old girl and married to her second husband, Bert Feinstein "the love of her life." Bert was chief of neurosurgery with his partner Grant Levin at Mount Zion Medical Center. I knew him as being innovative and highly respected. He was a good deal older that Dianne.

Dianne was determined to get to know all aspects of San Francisco. She even went to a porn movie with her good friend Merla Zellerbach. I am told that she even once stood on a corner in the Tenderloin (a seedy district) wearing a blond wig to see what happened to streetwalkers.

She taught me a lot about how elegant ladies liked to be treated after she became my patient at the suggestion of her father and her husband. Unfortunately her husband died after a long siege with colon cancer.

She ran for mayor unsuccessfully twice, but as noted earlier she was ready for the job when Moscone, the Mayor, was murdered. There were those who fought her because of her strict law and order attitudes. There was even a bomb placed near a window to her daughter's room. Fortunately, it fizzed. A bullet was shot through a window of her vacation house in Monterey. She made over the police force hiring fifty or more new officers and getting a new police chief.

She was a hero to so many for many things she did. She stopped her car often to help a person in distress even once to give mouth-to-mouth resuscitation. She often went to a fire to see if there was something she could do. She passed the toughest anti-gun law in the country. It banned handguns from most people. She supported gay rights. She was a friend of labor unions. She was strong on environmental protection. She fought for equal rights for women. She believed that good government should be helpful to all citizens.

Dianne had help from an unexpected source. San Francisco had a football team called the 49ers. It had not done well, had never made the playoffs. They even traded a quarterback to Oakland where he led Oakland to the Super Bowl. Edward DeBartolo Sr. gave the team to his son, Edward DeBartolo Jr. as a gift. The young Debartolo was anxious to make a name for himself. He fired the coach and hired a relatively unknown who had done fairly well at Stanford, Bill Walsh. His first major move was to hire Joe Montana who had been a backup quarterback at Notre Dame. He was not a high-rated pick because he seemed frail to other coaches, but Walsh saw things he wanted in Joe. Walsh loved football but believed the way the game was played should be changed. He developed a much more open style, later given the name "pacific coast." It took three years for Walsh to get what he wanted. He built a team with rejects who had the skills he was looking for. But then he began to win games and the city became interested. Dianne who knew nothing about football joined the crowd of fans and recovered the city box at the new football stadium "Candlestick." The 49ers beat the hated Dallas Cowboys, who had been called America's Team and God's Team, and then went on to win the Super Bowl in 1982. The city had evolved so that everyone was a fan. The celebration of the 1981 game against Dallas and the Super Bowl win caused the largest parade and celebration since the Japanese surrender. Dianne was the Mayor. Somehow she shared in reflected glory. She knew how important the team had become for her city.

In the 1980's, AIDS hit San Francisco. Kaposi's Sarcoma was the first obvious symptom. However, it was soon found that the immune system was almost entirely eliminated. A doctor working at San Francisco General Hospital, Paul Volberding, set up a ward for these patients, 5B. There was little that could be done except provide support.

Volberding went to Feinstein for support for his clinic and ward and research and asked for a large sum. He said, " She didn't blink an eye. She was completely responsive to whatever I asked from her." She had already seen our city devastated by loosing a major segment of the artistic community. My mother was a well-known interior decorator, and I knew many of her coworkers and friends. Most of them were lost as were leaders in many of the sections of the city that had given it beauty and charm. Even Bill Walsh's son was stricken. People not knowing much about how the

Feinstein 2000
The Democratic Senatorial Campaign Committee
Cordially invite you to attend
a dinner with

William Jefferson Clinton
President of the United States

at the Mark Hopkins Hotel
San Francisco

Friday, March 3, 2000
5:30 p.m. sharp

RSVP Card Enclosed
Inquiries to 415-395-8487

RSVP by February 28
Space limited

Paid for by "California Victory 2000," FEC #C00345876, a joint fundraising committee of the Democratic Senatorial Campaign Committee and Feinstein 2000.

disease spread began avoiding public places, restaurants, and various theaters. Dianne Feinstein rose to the challenge. She was a regular visitor to the ward at San Francisco Hospital and other areas that helped the ill, like Project Open Hand, which delivered food to the ill. The most important item in he San Francisco budget was money for AIDS care and research. Though New York City had twice as many with the disease, they did not spend half as much as San Francisco. Actually, San Francisco spent more on the problem than the entire United States under Ronald Reagan who felt that homosexuals were being punished.

Actually, he refused any specific support in spite of the repeated requests from his Surgeon General, C. Everett Koop. Thus, the search for understanding the disease was mostly left to San Francisco, with the heroic support of our mayor. Although we won, many thousands died who might have been saved if our country had the support of our President as much as San Francisco had the support of its mayor. In a way this dread disease brought the people together more than the 49ers.

I am told that Dianne insisted that Candlestick ballpark should be retrofitted to be earthquake proof. The park was full for the first game of the World Series. My son was in the stands. The strongest earthquake since 1906 hit. No one in the park was hurt. Dianne was my hero once again.

In 1990, Pete Wilson gave up his long tenure as United States Senator to become governor. He appointed John Seymour, another Republican, but there was an election in 1992 to fill out Wilson's term. Dianne won and thus was senior senator even though Barbara Boxer was elected at the same time. Dianne took over Wilson's seat in the Senate in the first row and she was on her way to be a hero again. She had told me once that she thought she was better qualified to be a governor than at senator, however, she learned her new job fast and her various accomplishments have been outstanding.

Particularly important was a gun control law against assault weapons that was a first. When an opponent suggested that she accept his amendment that would markedly weaken it, she replied that she held a dying man who had been shot and she would not yield.

She has been on a long list of important committees and often chair. Most recently as Chairman of the Intelligence Committee, she has dared to call out the C.I.A. on many areas where it had exceeded its rights. To many of us this has been a heroic action. She has been a leader in fuel economy standards, California desert protection, CALFED that is charged with solving the water problems in California, healthy forests, Lake Tahoe restoration, and San Francisco Bay Wetlands Restorations. We Californians honor all of them.

She has been a major player in insuring national security. She worked on crime victims' rights. Her bill banned assault weapons from 1994-2004. She has been a leader in various health issues, especially those of women. She started the Amber Alert. She is a hero over and over again.

She has been a leader in the United States Senate, and I hardly begin to tell of the wonders she has accomplished, She even has found time to remember my birthday and other events with personal notes and gifts.

She is for me, and so many others, a hero.

2.   CHARLES WILSON, M.D.

About 25 years ago, my wife Gwen had some neurological symptoms. An M.R.I. revealed a small tumor in her brain. It was alarming because some years before she had had a radical operation for an invasive melanoma. She had no evidence of recurrence until this time. She was scheduled for a biopsy of the brain lesion on the coming Monday. I looked at the film and thought the lesion did not look like most metastatic legions and I was worried about Gwen having what I considered a major procedure. I did what any smart San Francisco doctor would do. I called Charlie Wilson. He asked to see the films. He lived in Belvedere across the Bay. It was a weekend, but I checked out the films. I was told that they could not be taken out of the building. I selected the key films and returned the folder with the rest (breaking all rules). I got to

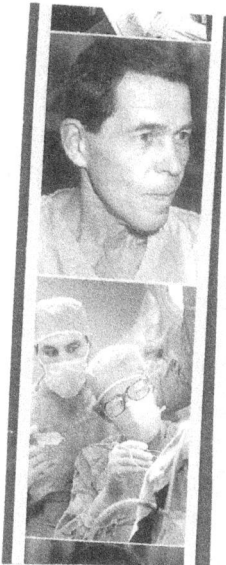

Charlie's lovely home in Belvedere. Francie, his lovely wife, met me to say that Charlie was on a run, but he would be home shortly. Charlie came in and without significant delay looked at the films. He thought the lesion looked benign; but to be sure, if a CT scan showed a calcium deposit the lesion would be benign and no biopsy would be needed. I arranged to get the scan. The lesion was calcified and the surgeon agreed that the surgery should be canceled. Charlie was my hero then and in many other ways. I could never understand why someone else had not thought of doing the CT.

When I was a medical student, Howard Nafziger was the chairman of neurosurgery. He had a national reputation and he was also chief of surgery. He retired in 1951 and died not long after. Edwin Boldry took his place. When I was an acting intern in 1943 I had the unpleasant experience of being second assistant during some of Doctor Boldry's surgeries. He drove me and others quite mad because of his painfully slow surgery. People in high position at U.C.S.F. seemed to recognize that and he was replaced by John Adams. But Adams was mostly interested in research. Between those two the department lost a great deal of activity. Then appeared on the scene the hero of the department, the medical school and a long line of trainees, Charles Wilson. It did not take long before a major percentage of admissions to the University of California Medical Center were patients of Charles Wilson. I think you should know how one man made so much difference.

Doctor Wilson was born in 1929 in Missouri. His mother was of Cherokee heritage, a direct descendant of a Cherokee chief. Charles from an early age was a perfectionist. His self-discipline continued to mark him. When is father died, his mother sent him to military school which appealed to him. There he enjoyed sports like equestrian jumping and football. When he went to high school, he continued to love sports, and even though relatively small, became the captain of the basketball team. When he graduated from high school, Charles was offered a football scholarship and an academic scholarship at Tulane. While there he decided to be a doctor rather than to be a clergyman which profession he had considered. He was an outstanding medical student and remained in New Orleans to do a residency in Neurosurgery. His second wife was from New Orleans, and it was good for them to develop there with their two children. Because he did extremely well and was building a reputation he was offered a chance to be in charge of neurosurgery at the University of Kentucky that he accepted. There he developed what had been part of the surgery department to be a respected full department.

In 1968 Charlie was offered the chairmanship of neurosurgery at the University of California Medical School in San Francisco. This was unusual because he was only 38. The offer was well deserved. He was not only a skilled surgeon who was driven toward perfection there but in all other aspects of his chosen life's work. He had become a superior neuropathologist, and a superb administrator winning the admiration and love of his trainees. He was modest but demanding of perfection that led to his becoming a hero to all of us who know him.

In 1999, Malcolm Gladwell wrote a memorable piece in *The New Yorker* about Wilson. He started his article saying that Charlie had just performed his one-thousand, nine hundred and eighty-seventh trans-sphenoidal resection of a pituitary tumor. Now this was remarkable when you consider he had done many other operations in his ten years at U.C.S.F. This operation Charlie did in as little as twenty five minutes while other neurosurgeons who I have known might take as long as three hours. The approach is through a canal only a little larger than a centimeter in diameter starting beneath the upper lip. The pituitary gland is located in a dangerous area where the slightest error by the surgeon can be catastrophic. But Wilson was perfection in concentration and coordination. Gladwell compared him with other technical geniuses like Yo-Yo Ma, Wayne Gretsky, the professional hockey star and the great baseball hitters and pitchers.

"What sets physical geniuses apart from other people is not merely being able to do something but knowing what to do—their capacity to pick up on subtle patterns that others generally miss. This is what we mean when we say that great athletes have a "feel" for the game, or that they "see" the court or the field in a special way. Neurosurgeons say that when the very best surgeons operate they always know where they are going and they mean that the Charlie Wilsons of this world possess that special feel, an ability to calculate the diversions and to factor in the interruptions when

faced with a confusing mass of blood and tissue."
(Gladwell)

Though he had been an outstanding doctor
from the start, he did not reach this sort of perfection
without careful study and practice including work on
cadavers. He also believed that good surgeons should
be in good physical condition. His efforts in that
direction were legendary and to my way of thinking
perhaps excessive. He and I agreed that those we
trained should keep themselves in shape. We had them
use the stairs instead of elevators whenever possible. If
they had a break, the university had a gym and
swimming pool access the street

Why is this man a hero? He was a major
contributor to the progression of the University of
California Medical School from a very good school to
being one of the very best in the United States and the
rest of the world. In all the years that I practiced my
specialty I knew no one who trained such a large group
of first-rate specialists. More important: He improved
more lives than any other surgeon I have known, his
patients.

Mr. Sanchez, French Regimental Croix de Guerre,
Odette LePendu
July 10, 2013

3.   ODETTE LePENDU

If you were to meet Odette LePendu today in 2014, you like me, might find it difficult to believe that this pleasant little lady, not more that five feet tall, is a hero of the resistance against the Germans in World War II.

Odette's parents moved to San Francisco in the twenties. They had heard good things about San Francisco from their relatives, the Boudin family who owned and operated a famous bakery in the city. Odette was born in the French Hospital there 91 years ago. She grew up as a typical American girl, though she spoke with a slight but real French accent. Her last school in San Francisco was Presidio Jr. High where she completed the first part of the ninth grade when her parents decided to return to France. Hardly settled in Paris they were confronted by the fact that the Nazis were overwhelming the French army. They decided to move to Vichy France to a small city, Caylus, that is 44 km. north of Mantauban. There she was horrified to see that the Gestapo had the real power. The first evidence of that was when some men accused of being sympathetic to the resistance were hanged in front of the Prefecture and left there until they rotted. Her parents sent her to Toulouse where she spent two years in Lycée. Her parents decided to move her back home being worried about her in Toulouse that was in

German territory. By the time she rejoined her parents she was 18.

One day, a friend of her family asked her to take a message on her bicycle. She was a bit fearful, because German soldiers in the area often confiscated bicycles. If the owner refused to give up his or her bicycle they were often shot. On the other hand, Odette was a small teenager and she was not bothered. Actually, that had been a trial run. She was offered a chance to join the French Resistance and she accepted. The local faction was the Mithridate network, one of the most important underground networks of more than 1,600 agents who gathered military intelligence in support of Allied operations.

Because Odette was fluent in English and French, she soon became a liaison and an interpreter for radio operators of the Resistance. One of the German priorities was to destroy any communications with the Allies, and radio operations were prime target at all times. That being so, transmitters were frequently moved and hidden. Odette tells of riding her bicycle through enemy lines with a transmitter hidden in her basket. The Germans did not suspect a young girl on a bicycle, at least not for a while. On one fateful day Odette volunteered to hide the radio transmitter that her unit was using in her home. Somehow the Gestapo found this out and arrested her. She was taken to Toulouse. She was interrogated repeatedly for days. She could not communicate with anyone. Her mother was determined to find her. She made innumerable calls to people in authority whom she knew: French, Swiss, American, and even German. In a week she was able to get Odette released mainly through the influence of the Swiss Legation. Odette states that the Nazis were about to ship her off to Germany. Odette moved out of France because she was known there. However, she was still able to work for the Resistance until the end of the war, which fortunately came soon.

She returned to the Unite States in 1947. In San Francisco, she met her husband François. They raised two sons. Françoise had been a merchant seaman during the war. He and Odette later helped form a group of veterans who developed a project to restore a Liberty Ship, the SS *Jeremiah O'Brien* that was tied up in San Francisco and one of the last of its kind. Their goal was to land it in Normandy in 1994, the fiftieth anniversary of D-Day where it was preserved as a memorial to those who provided the supplies to the invasion of Europe.

In 2003, the French awarded the Legion of Honor to Odette for her bravery during the war. It is unusual for a woman to get that honor. She continues even now in her 90's to find people she considers heroes, and I think she helped find me to get the Legion of Honor from President Sarkozy when he came briefly to the United States in 2007. She is a member of the American Society of French Legion of Honor and often has written for it. More recently, the French Government decided that Odette deserved a much higher rank, Officer of the French Legion of Honor. There are few of that rank and it took a time for a person of that level to pin that important and beautiful medal on Odette, a true hero, on July 10, 2013.

Sam Ladar

4.   SAM LADAR

Sam Ladar was a hero to me, but more important, he was a hero to our community because of his unstinting efforts for charities and community projects. He was often the chairman who performed in a superior way always prepared and on time. He was a source of strength for the Mount Zion Hospital and Medical Center.

Sam Ladar was an orphan, but he had support systems from family and friends. When he arrived at the University of California in Berkeley, he became popular and even a subject of a successful novel. He was a talented basketball player. Even though he was the shortest man on the team he became captain. His last Big Game against Stanford was for the championship. Ernie Nevers was the captain for Stanford. The game was tied with almost no time left. Sam was fouled. Sam pumped up. His shot hit the basket rim and bounced over the backboard. The game went into overtime. Stanford got the tipoff. Sam stole the ball, fought his way up the court and sank the winning shot. The stands went wild. He did not stay around for bows. He grabbed his girlfriend, Sylvia, and cleared out. That was the sort of man that he was. He was a hero then and to me and many others for the rest of his life.

When I was a senior at Cal, my father gave me his membership at Lake Merced Golf Club. I was a fair to good golfer, but I did not have much time to play. However, one of the people I got to play with was a young lawyer named Sam Ladar. At first I did not know much about him except what I knew about his impressive golfing ability, much better than mine, and his obvious knowledge and camaraderie. When I returned from the war, we took up golfing together some; however, I had to devote most of my time to residency training. Finally, when I went into practice, I needed a lawyer. I knew two other lawyers, Ben Lehrer and John Golden, both of whom took on high profile cases, but I decided that Sam was the man I needed, and it was an excellent choice.

By that time, Sam had begun to have an established position in our community. He worked with great energy doing a variety of services pro bono. I learned more and more about him. He went to U.C. Berkeley and later to Boalt Hall, the prestigious law school at U.C.

After I had been in practice awhile, I had a partner and moved close to Mount Zion Hospital where I did most of my work. This made it possible for me to play a bit more golf. My handicap rapidly dropped to a respectable 12. Now, I was free to play with Sam and other good players like my friend Les Fink without feeling completely outclassed. Golfing together, Sam and I developed an even closer friendship. When a new clubhouse was built, we asked that our lockers be next to each other.

Pauline (my secretary since I started practice) was pregnant, so I hired a young woman who was efficient and well liked by my patients. After a year or so, she was engaged to marry a young man from a good family in the Midwest. My wife and I bought her a silver tray from Gumps for a wedding gift. When I hired a new person to take her place, the new woman, Kathy, in checking the books, found that the woman before her had obviously been stealing cash that was paid into the office. She figured that the amount was about $15,000, which was a lot in those days. I called Sam. He said that I should meet him at once at the District Attorney's office. I said that I had patients to see. He said that I should arrange for them to be seen, but that he would meet me as soon as possible in the DA's office.

The district attorney found out almost at once that my former employee had left the state and had moved to Michigan with her new husband. He said that it was impossible for us to extradite her from there to California, however, if she ever came to California to let him know. I found the address of my former employee and wrote to her, but I got no answer.

I had just about written off the money I was owed when one day one of my patients told me she had seen my former employee in Southern California apparently visiting her mother for Thanksgiving. I called Sam who contacted the district attorney. On the day before Thanksgiving, he had the woman arrested and put in jail. Her husband called me, indignant that I had taken such an action. He even said if he had known I was going to be so mean he would have paid the money owed me. He suggested he pay me the money over a period of time. I said the whole matter was out of my hands, and that he would have to deal with the district attorney in San Francisco. The next day, even though it was a holiday, the DA called me to ask if I would be happy just to get the money with no further action by him, Mr. Ladar, or me. I said that would be fine. A couple of days later I got a cashier's check for the exact amount that had been stolen. I give full credit in that matter to Sam, who was respected by the district attorney, who in turn acted efficiently probably not for me so much as for Sam. So, then Sam was certainly my hero.

Over the years, when I had major decisions to make, I usually consulted my parents. I felt that my father was very practical and knew about the business world. After my Dad died in 1971, Sam became my major consultant on matters non-medical. He was the most ethical person I have ever known, and his guidance was invaluable. I think the only bill I ever got from him was when he wrote a partnership agreement for me. That agreement proved to be most valuable.

Sam's wife, Sylvia, became a patient of mine. She had been a patient of Alice Maxwell who had recently retired. Doctor Maxwell was one of the very best, and I felt honored to have been chosen. She was a perfect partner for Sam. They had been close since their years in college.

Sam and I began to play golf together regularly on Saturdays. We had a wonderful foursome with Jack Davis and Stan Breyer. Our lockers were close together.

Samuel Ladar — S.F. Lawyer, Civic Leader

By Bill Wallace
Chronicle Staff Writer

Samuel A. Ladar, 87, a prominent San Francisco attorney who served as president of the city's Board of Education and Police Commission during the 1960s, died Monday at his home in Pacific Heights.

Mr. Ladar was noted for his lifelong service with educational, religious and charitable organizations.

"He worked tirelessly in the community for the things he believed in, and he wasn't afraid of the leadership role," said his son, Jerrold, in a speech to the Boalt Hall Alumni Association during ceremonies honoring Mr. Ladar last June. "About the only thing he wasn't any good at was blowing his own horn."

Mr. Ladar was born in the Mother Lode community of Jackson. He moved to San Francisco at a young age and attended Laguna Honda Grammar School and the High School of Commerce in the city, earning money in his spare time as a newsboy for the Examiner and Call-Bulletin newspapers.

He received his undergraduate degree from the University of California at Berkeley in 1926 and graduated from Boalt Hall in 1928.

After law school, Mr. Ladar joined the law firm of Steinhart, Feigenbaum and Goldberg. He was with the firm for 62 years, ultimately becoming a full partner.

Mr. Ladar spent years in government service. He was a member of the San Francisco school board from 1960 to 1967 and was the board's president in 1962. He was appointed to the Police Commission in 1967 and was its president in 1968.

He was a member of a crime task force from 1968 until 1971, and also served on two state commissions: the California Commission on Certificated Employment Practices and the postwar Committee on Resettlement of Displaced Persons.

Mr. Ladar also found time to work with a variety of charitable, religious and professional organizations, including the Boalt Hall alumni committee, United Way, Mount Zion Hospital, the American Jewish Committee, the Jewish Welfare Federation of San Francisco, Marin and the Peninsula.

Mr. Ladar is survived by his wife, Sylvia; his son, Jerrold; and his daughter-in-law, Joyce. He is also survived by two grandsons, Jeffrey B. and Jonathan M. Ladar, and by several nieces and nephews.

A public memorial service will be held at 4 p.m. Thursday at Temple Emanu-El. Mr. Ladar's family has requested that any contributions in his memory be made to the American Jewish Committee, the Jewish Community Federation Endowment Fund, or the John Kerner Cancer Fund at Mt. Zion Hospital.

We played our hearts out in competition for a few dollars, but we had great times.

Sam developed cancer of the pancreas for which there was no treatment. But he kept going as long as he could, and I recall a pleasant dinner we had with him and Sylvia at Perry's only a few nights before he died. He never complained.

About a year before he died, Sam and I were playing golf as a team. He was beginning to loose strength. We were on the last hole. Our match was tied. We were playing for our usual large sums (four or five dollars were at stake). A large trap protected the green. To win, Sam would have to clear the trap but not be too far from the hole. He selected his club and carefully wiped the blade. He took a couple of practice swings. He then made a perfect shot that ended close enough to make the putt and win the match for our team. One of our opponents knocked the ball away and said, "That's good Sam." Sam said, "You shouldn't have done that. You take away the fun. You take away meeting the challenge." He put the ball down and made the putt.

These events, though almost a lifetime apart, tell you a great deal about Sam. He faced the challenges of life with intensity whether they involved sports, his profession, or volunteer work, and even committees (for which he was always well prepared). He faced death that way too.

He didn't expect anyone to give him anything, even a putt, and certainly not kudos. He probably would have been embarrassed by all this today.

He was an inspiration and a father figure for me, and I am sure for many others. He and Sylvia made the greatest team I've ever known.

If I may borrow from our liturgy: As long as I live, when I am on a golf course, when I hear a lucid argument, when I see a graceful athlete, most important when I must make an ethical decision I, like many of you, will think of Sam, my hero.

Barbara Bass Bakar

5.   BARBARA BASS BAKAR

To hundreds of underserved children, and to so many others, and me, Barbara Bass Bakar is a hero.

If you were to ask Barbara Bass Bakar what was the most important thing she has ever done, I think she would say that was the formation of Achieve. Other people might say that she was one of the first women in our country to reach the highest levels of a retail business. Especially considering at 36 she was already chairman and chief executive of the I Magnin Company. But, that was just a start.

"Achieve is a year-round, four-year college preparatory program for underserved students from low-income families. Over 70 students currently participate in this scholarship and enrichment program and attend single-gender parochial high schools." That hardly tells the story.

Barbara founded this program in 1997 and has invested her time, executive experience, love of children, and respect for the advantages of education. She has provided after-school classrooms, teachers, computers, and supervision. Barbara gets to know her students and their families. She is willing to talk with parents and to follow her students to be sure they hold up their end of the bargain even when the students go on to college.

In almost every instant her students graduate from college. This is amazing when you consider that they are usually the first in their family to go to college. Her students are given help in selecting colleges and they have been enrolled in major universities. They have a remarkable record of receiving scholarship support from the schools they choose. Their success after graduation is remarkable.

The students are selected on "the basis of academic achievement, leadership potential and motivation to excel. They are expected to maintain a 3.0 GPA while taking rigorous course loads. Active parental support and participation are required."

Barbara makes a big effort to find good internships for the students to have in the summertime. She wants internships that enhance the particular goals the student has. For a number of years I had one of Achieve's students do a summer internship in my laboratory at Mount Zion. We were working in cancer research with a special goal to find cures for cancer. To my pleasant surprise I found that by the end of the summer most of these high school students who reported to my group each week on their work in the laboratory knew more about cancer research techniques than most first-year medical students.

I remember that on another summer an Achieve student who worked in my lab was remarkably effective and the reports she gave at our weekly meetings were unusually mature. She was accepted at a first-rate New England university with a full scholarship for four years. Barbara found out that she had only one dress so she took the girl to good stores and outfitted her for the first time in her life. It is easy for you to see why Barbara was a hero to these kids.

Each year each student writes a Senior Reflection. It is a joy to read them for they reflect gratefulness and ambition. Equally, they reflect love and respect for Barbara and what she has made possible for them.

Barbara graduated from Smith College with a first-rate record in her studies and her chosen major, economics. She began her career in retail in 1972 as an assistant buyer at Federated's Burdines Division in Miami. Though she had been accepted at Harvard Business School, she was persuaded to work for Macy's where she spent 5 years in California as a buyer for furniture and ready-to-wear. She did an outstanding job showing remarkable taste with lower cost products than had been Macy's practice. She was made division manager. She joined Bloomingdale's in 1980 as operating vice president for branch store merchandising. In 1985, she was promoted to executive vice president and merchandise manager. At the age of 36, she became chairman and chief executive of San Francisco-based I. Magnin & Company.

But now she had married Gerson Bakar and she felt that she was done being a retail executive. She resigned. She and Gerson formed a major foundation and had served on many boards including Starbucks, Bebe, and Duty Free Shops. Now there was time to start Achieve!

Barbara and Gerson have together become community heroes for their major support of the University of California particularly its medical school and innumerable community projects, as well as for establishing the Achieve program.

Barbara is a hero to all of us who are interested in the cancer program at U.C.S.F. An annual event, Raising Hope, that she developed and chaired has raised a significant amount of money for the cancer program. With her husband Gerson, she provided two distinguished professorships in the cancer program: one in Cancer Genetics and one in Cancer Biology. They also sponsored a fellowship program at U.C. Berkeley that supports innovative research. Nancy Pelosi has honored her for her work in health care. Barbara received the U.C.S.F. Medal, the highest honor U.C.S.F. can offer, for her contributions to the university's health-care mission.

Frosting on the cake—Barbara is always great to look at.

6.   HERBERT TRAUT

I first met Doctor Traut when he interviewed me to be an intern in his Department of Obstetrics and Gynecology at the University of California Medical School in San Francisco. I was to be his first house staff member to be appointed by Doctor Traut as the new chief. He was only the second chairman of a fully organized department at U.C.S.F. His predecessor, Frank Lynch, had been chairman for close to thirty years. Traut was a superb choice. At the time we first met I knew little about him. However, over the years I learned that he was probably the most important hero I would know in my life.

He was born in Muscotah, Kansas on April 3, 1894. He was the son of a Congregational minister, the Reverend George Albert Traut and Frances McCormick Traut. He was proud of that heritage. After his secondary education in Sheridan Wyoming, he enrolled in Whitman College in Walla Walla Washington from which he received a B.S. degree in 1917. World War I had begun and he felt it his duty to enlist after he graduated. Being a conscientious student he achieved the rank of 2nd Lieutenant in the field artillery of the United States Army. As was common at that time he was transferred from the A.E.F. to the 128th French Artillery Regiment, Battery D. There in his first battle he was awarded the French Croix de Guerre with Palm. This was an unusual event for few Americans received that military honor. He had suffered a leg wound in that action on June 14, 1918. That wound troubled him for the rest of his life. In spite of the wound, he continued with his job. The citation reads.

"During a German attack, having one of their guns blown to pieces and all the gunners killed, the second platoon of this battery, thanks to the energy of 2nd Lieutenant Herbert F. Traut, continued the barrage fire until their ammunition was exhausted. By doing

Prof. Herbert Traut

so, they were able to shelter our first line, situated in front of them, from enemy infantry attack."

He also was awarded an American Purple Heart. Interestingly, though I knew him for the rest of his life, he never mentioned the military experience to me even when we both talked as veterans.

Following the war, he enrolled in Johns Hopkins School of Medicine where he received his M.D. in 1923. He married a charming woman, Marjorie Wentworth immediately after graduating. In later years he preached deferring marriage until training was complete. Marriage did not keep him from becoming one of the best-qualified young doctors of his time. He served a year of internship in surgery, a year in plastic surgery under John Stage Davis, a father of that specialty, three years of gynecology, and two years of obstetrics at Hopkins. Johns Hopkins was considered the best school of obstetrics and gynecology at that time. They were two separate departments. He then won a traveling fellowship in Europe. He studied in England, Scandinavia, and Germany. During those postgraduate years he worked with some of the great doctors of that time: Howard Kelley was considered the best gynecological surgeon. Thomas Cullen was a great surgeon. J. Witridge Williams the author of a major textbook on obstetrics. Perhaps most important, he worked with Robert Meyer in Berlin. Meyer was considered the world's greatest gynecologic and obstetric pathologist, particularly in gynecology. At that time he had a profound influence on Traut that later led to one of medical history's great discoveries.

In 1931, so well prepared, he was invited to join the faculty of Cornell Medical College as an associate professor. While there, he met and worked with Doctor George N. Papanicolaou, a professor of clinical anatomy.

Papaniculaou having become interested in the cytology of the estrous cycle in animals developed a technique for staining smears of cells that helped to differentiate different types of cells. He decided he would use this technique on women. While doing this he began to notice some unusual cells and groups of cells. He asked Traut to look at some of his slides. Traut pointed out to him and he agreed that these cells looked like those of cancer. They published a monograph illustrating their findings.

At that point Doctor Traut was invited to be the chairman of the Department of Obstetrics and Gynecology at U.C.S.F. That was the point at which I met him.

He rapidly became one of the most highly respected professors at U.C.S.F. His second year course in obstetrics and gynecology became a medical school classic. Seniors taking their overall examination prior to graduation scored best in Obstetrics and Gynecology during his tenure and the students often selected him as the best teacher in the school. His house staff learned of his demand for superior patient care and devotion to duty. He helped those of us who needed financial help and never asked to be repaid. He taught me to develop a fund from which I could support residents or research. He had told me that he did not want me to set my fees in practice according to the financial position of the husband, as was the practice in San Francisco at that time. He said that patients or their husbands might ask why they were not charged more for his professional care. He said to respond that I had a fund that I use for education and research and if the patient or her husband wanted to contribute to that fund, it would be greatly appreciated. Later I followed this lead with considerable success. His fund continues, supported by Ed Hill one of his favorite residents.

After the War, I had the good fortune to act as his assistant in his lectures that were illustrated with slides that at that time were large glass. He told me to make slides of typical cancer cells in smears and pair them with tissue samples. No one at U.C.S.F. had made such slides. I found a technician who had been asked to make slides of blood cells. So, in afterhours we did our work. I had a beautiful small German camera that we fastened to the eyepiece of her excellent microscope that had been focused on high power (using oil immersion). After many trials with focus and lighting we were able to make excellent slides that are still in existence. These slides became important in Doctor Traut's heroic proving that smears were a valid and useful addition to the medical armamentarium. They made possible the early diagnosis of cervical and uterine cancers and even pre-cancer changes. He had to overcome marked resistance from many pathologists who thought tissue was the only answer to diagnosis. Early in my private practice, the American Cancer Society with Doctor Traut's blessing sent me around the State of California to speak about the value of the smears. In the end, Doctor Traut won that battle. The vaginal smears, by finding disease early, have saved thousands of lives each year. For a while they were called Papanicalaou-Traut but eventually the name was shortened to "Pap." During a major illness, Doctor Traut was replaced by Ernest Page, a man who had been in practice, who did research and gave good talks. Most of us at U.C. felt that he was not up to the challenge that Doctor Traut had established.

How many heroes can one think of like Herbert Traut who saved so many women from a truly terrible disease? I will always be grateful for his teaching me how to carry on his work.

7.   ALAN MARGOLIS

Until the 1950's the disease of the newborn, erythroblastosis fetalis of the newborn, was a major problem causing many deaths. Alan Margolis had the courage to increase the knowledge of erythroblastosis while facing criticism for the risks he took facing malpractice liability. I thought Alan was heroic in what he did for our specialty.

Erythroblastosis is a disease that has been known for generations, but it was not understood until the 1940's. When I was in training, at first, what we knew about blood was that there were four types: A, B, AB, and O. But in attempts to cross-match blood, we found matches that we expected to work did not. At that point hematologists at U.C. Medical School, San Francisco, led by Stacy Metier M.D., felt there must be subgroups. They found one which they called the Rh factor. That name was chosen because their research had been done with Rhesus monkeys. If the unborn child of a mother without Rh factor, called "Rh negative," had a baby with the factor, called "Rh positive"(which had come from the father), her immune system would develop antibodies to Rh as small amounts of the baby's blood would cross the placenta. Her next pregnancy would be complicated by her immunity destroying the fetus' red blood cells. This caused anemia and therefore swelling of tissues often leading to death or severe illness of the fetus. Blood tests to measure the severity of the immunity were developed with the plan to deliver the baby by inducing labor or even by Caesarean section before it was too ill; and then to transfuse it with Rh-negative blood. The plan had many failures either delivering the baby too soon or too late.

A doctor in England thought measuring the density of the amniotic fluid might be a better way to evaluate the fetus, but he could not make his idea work.

Alan Margolis

A doctor in New Zealand, Lily, thought the idea was a good one and he made it work.

Alan visited with Lily. Lily had found that he could detect with some certainty the severity of the baby's disease by studying the optical density of the amniotic fluid. He created a curve from which severity of anemia could be quite accurately determined. Alan thought we should try to duplicate the technique. We found that one of the medical centers in southern California had tried and failed. We collected amniotic fluid by inserting a needle into the amniotic cavity in what we felt was a safe area. This was a new procedure for us. We took the fluid to our laboratory at Mount Zion Hospital where there was a visiting expert who understood what we were trying to do. We found that evaluating the baby using optical density related to the breakdown products of fetal blood worked much better than studying the immune reaction. We began doing the test for ourselves and for the University of California workers who could not get the proper results. We could now be more certain about the severity of the baby's disease. More were saved. No one criticized Alan for his pioneering move. However, he faced the risk of being attacked if something went wrong.

The next step was to try to save babies that were affected severely but too immature to deliver. Lily decided to transfuse a baby while it was still in the uterus by putting a needle through the abdomen into the baby's abdomen and injecting Rh-negative blood which he hoped would be absorbed and utilized by the baby. It was. So Alan with me as an assistant thought we should try to repeat the procedure. We knew that no one in the U.S. had ever tried that, and if there was some major problem, we could be sued for malpractice.

Our first patient has the wife of a well-known politician. She had lost three babies to erythroblastosis, even her first. This baby we transfused while still in the mother's uterus. It survived. I think Alan and I absorbed a lot of X-ray doing this. Ultrasound was not yet available. When our next try failed we decided future transfusion be done at U.C.S.F. where some success was achieved. That was the start of intrauterine surgery.

Shots which prevented the mother's allergic reaction were developed at Columbia Medical Center called Rhogam. Those shots eliminated the problem of erythroblastosis if the shots were administered early in pregnancy when the mother was Rh negative and the father was positive.

Alan Margolis was a credit to our profession. He was a favorite teacher both at Mount Zion and at U.C.S.F. He was interested not only in being a good practitioner but also in advancing the cause of women and improving our knowledge of pregnancy. These talents eventually led to his becoming full-time on the university faculty.

8.   WALTER S. NEWMAN

Walt was a hero to the men he trained and fought with in World War II and again to those and many other veterans of our most recent wars when he established a program to help veterans of all wars but especially the most recent. He is a hero to those who have to deal with brain tumors in their children and those who try to find cures when he set up a fund for those purposes. He was a good citizen.

Walt was a good friend of mine late in his life, but I had known him quite well for most of our lives. He went to public schools including U.C. Berkeley where he took Army R.O.T.C. It was natural for him to join the army as World War II began. He was well liked and a born leader. He rapidly advanced in the army to the rank of captain in the 35th Infantry Division in which I also served. When our division landed on Omaha Beach as part of the invasion force, Walt was a company commander. At that time most of the officers were from the National Guard or regular army. Walt had trained his men well and they liked and respected him. It was natural for Walt to lead his men in our first major battle. The battle was brutal. We had not been trained to deal with the problems that we would face in the hedgerows of Normandy. Walt had a severe chest wound. Our division fell back a bit to regroup. I went

to search for Walt and found that in spite of a
dangerous wound his aid men had evacuated him alive.
Fortunately, it was possible to transport him to
England. I wrote my mother of all of this and she called
his mother who had not heard the good news that Walt
had survived. He received the Purple Heart medal. I
am sure he was entitled to the Combat Infantry Medal
and with it a Bronze Star. I do not know why he did
not get those two. Much later the president of France
awarded him the French Legion of Honor. Walt was a
hero to his men and he met with the survivors many
times after the war.

Walter S. Newman

"After the war, Walt returned to the central
valley town of Newman California which had been
founded by his Grandfather." He managed various
interests there. When he married Ellen Magnin his life
changed and centered in San Francisco where he went
to work for his father-in-law. Cyril Magnin owned and
operated successful group of retail stores, Joseph
Magnin.

Walter and Ellen raised a family of three sons. They had the devastating loss of one of their sons to a brain tumor. Walt again was a hero to many when he founded the National Brain Tumor Foundation.

Because of his interest in civic affairs he joined many community organizations and due to his leadership abilities he usually became president or chairman.

He came to me one day and pointed out that though the veterans in the various wars we had fought since World War II had various potential rewards, they often did not know how to take advantage of those rewards. He noted that this was especially true at the City College of San Francisco. That was so because that school was one of the least expensive in the country and most of the veterans had limited funds. There was a great difference to the veterans of World War II who had more ease in taking advantage of the Veteran's Bill of Rights. The City College offered minimal help. So with the money Walt and I provided and the cooperation that Walt obtained for his plan, there was established the Veterans Resource Center, which served as a meeting place for student veterans. It also was to help veterans' awareness of veterans' opportunities and to help them utilize those.

Two rooms were provided. One firm gave a number of computers, another gave carpeting. IKEA said, "Send a truck over and take anything you think you need." So now there was a computer lab, information about available resources, couches, a table to do homework, and free coffee. The mission was "to help foster a sense of community among student veterans." The center was an immediate success and soon additional offices were added for various consultants including psychiatric. Walt was a hero to those thousands and the center was named after him after his death.

The president of France more recently, joined many more in calling Walt a hero when he awarded him "The Chevalier de la Legion d'Honneur" for his wartime services.

9.   HELEN ROWAN

Certainly, my patients had a profound effect on me and my life as a doctor. One of the first was Helen Rowan. For me and many others she was a hero.

Before she came to San Francisco, Helen had gone to Mills College, the State Department, and then the Carnegie Corporation. She was referred to me by Julius Krevans, who at the time was professor medicine at U.C.S.F. Helen had no major gynecological problem when I first saw her. Early on, she impressed me as being an unusual woman. I liked her enthusiasm, her sensitivity, her honesty, and sense of humor. She had an aliveness which was refreshing in an otherwise busy day. She was a crusader who could be furious at the injustices of the world and shared my hatred of the abortion situation in our country. She had written a highly important article on the discrimination and injustices suffered by Mexican-Americans in the United States.

I had not seen Helen for a while because she was young, and I thought that visiting my office twice a year was adequate. During one of those intervals, she developed pelvic symptoms. I was on my first trip to Europe and my new partner Alan Margolis saw her and noted an abnormality in her pelvis. He looked through my notes and found that this was a new finding, and he advised that she should have surgery to determine the nature of this mass. At the time, there was no ultrasound, no CT, no MRI. X-rays were of minimal value. Helen decided that she would like to postpone any surgery until I returned from Europe.

When I checked in at my office, one of the first things that Alan told me was that there was some sort of a mass in Helen's pelvis. I got her in at once and, of course, noted the change in her pelvic examination. With her approval, I scheduled surgery after suitable workup. She had a wild ovarian cancer. Though its total mass was not great, it involved all of the neighboring organs. I did an extensive operation, removing all visible tumor, the uterus, both tubes and ovaries, and the omentum (a large fatty pad in the abdomen, a frequent place for cancer to spread). She was then treated with irradiation and chemotherapy under the best available supervision. Sadly, the tumor recurred a few months later. Now, I learned what a wonderful woman she was, and I learned a great deal about relationships with patients.

She amazed me. She treated her cancer not as a bitter, unjust blow of fate, but merely as a monumental inconvenience. I got in the habit of stopping by her apartment on my way home from my office, even though there was little I could do. I think she was looking after me. She had a serenity, a strength, a balance, and wisdom that to that point in my life were unmatched. Here was a person who could be furious at the injustices of the world, but did not view her prolonged illness as unjust. The physically debilitating effects of her cancer and its treatment did not manifest themselves in anger, fear, or self pity.

With all of her problems, she continued to live an active, involved life. Often, when I stopped by, she had friends visiting. She got out and explored San Francisco. She had a special love affair with the sights, sounds, and smells of the city. She would go out to dinner with friends, though often she could eat very little. She never lost her sense of humor, particularly when amused at herself. She had comments about hospital gowns and the paperwork involved in getting treated. She often poked fun at the attitudes, the words, or the deeds of a particularly pretentious, condescending, or arrogant politician, bureaucrat, doctor, or other public figure.

I was amazed at the numbers of important people that assembled at her apartment and later at her bedside. People like John Gardner, her former boss, traveled regularly from Washington to visit with her. Julius Krevans who became dean and then chancellor at U.C.S.F. found time to visit with her. There was no great solemnity. They asked her opinions. They talked about their problems. She was a great listener. She paid attention. Soon, I began telling her about my problems with patients or office management. Somehow, she was able to make me smile.

Even in her illness, she was generous in her friendships—almost to a fault. One day, I found that a son of a friend had put his sleeping bag in the corner of her living room for a while. I know that she put up bail for a young friend who got picked up for throwing a joint out of his car in the presence of local police. She took a great interest in me and my professional efforts and encouraged me to keep on working with cancer. She was sure that I would find ways to improve cure rates.

When she died two years after surgery, she left a letter for me. In it, she thanked be for my care and friendship and she insisted that I not feel guilty for not having cured her. She set up a fund in my name: It contained five thousand dollars, which was a significant sum at that time. It was to be known as the JOHN A. KERNER FOUNDATION. To quote the document:

a) The purpose of the Foundation shall be to advance the practice of medicine in the field of obstetrics and gynecology, as well as to establish teaching funds for fellows and students in that field.
b) The foregoing enumeration purposes shall not be construed as a limitation upon the use of the funds of the Foundation by Dr. Kerner, but he shall in his sole discretion, expend the funds for any purpose in the field of obstetrics and gynecology.

That gift and that document changed my life. I never earned huge sums of money in part because I gave a good deal of pro bono time to the university and to teaching at Mount Zion. My various partners sometimes objected to that. Patients heard of my fund and began to give generously to it. Now at the later part of my life, I find that the fund started by Helen has provided over four million dollars to various projects originally in teaching but recently more in cancer. Helen's donation fit in with the plan that was suggested by Doctor Traut. At this point, my interest in cancer diagnosis and treatment got a major stimulus. I hoped that I could learn to protect women from the terrible disease that Helen had; but if they got it, I hoped to help develop a cure.

She also left me a beautiful carved wooden head that she had obtained in Africa when she worked for the Carnegie Corporation. It is in a prominent place in my home, and when I see it I think of her.

John Gardner told me a story about her and her candor. He was interviewing her for a job at the Carnegie Corporation. After carefully reviewing her application, he noted the unusual number of prior employers. He asked: "Would you say you are a restless person, Miss Rowan?" Her answer was immediate and to the point: "I am restless, but not irresponsible." She was hired on the spot.

There was a Greek of old who noted that we can't be sure of a man's character and education until we know how he dies. She taught me about this and how to relate to the dying. She also started me on the long journey to find a cure for cancer. She was a hero to me, and to so many others.

Herma Hill Kay

10. HERMA HILL KAY

My specialty is obstetrics and gynecology. Naturally, I developed a great interest in non-medical problems. It has always seemed important to me to understand what is going on in my patients lives for certainly that might be a factor in their health and welfare. So, I immediately had special interest in my new patient Herma Hill Kay. She was a faculty member of Boalt Hall, the prestigious law school of the University of California, Berkeley. I had known Boalt graduates, but I had never heard of there being a female faculty member. She became a hero to me and especially to an extremely large group of women and to the many law students she has taught and teaches to this day. The fact that she became dean of Boalt Hall law school underlines what I plan to tell you. Women at the time she reached that level were rare everywhere in the world.

From the time I first knew her, Herma has been devoted to "telling the story of the entry of women professors into the previously all-male law school world during the twentieth century." That is only part of her story.

She likes to tell of her inspiration to enter the world of law. A favorite grammar school teacher told her that even though a girl would have a tough time being a lawyer, if Herma were her daughter she would vote for that profession. Herma obviously did not forget that. She graduated magna cum laude with departmental distinction in English from Southern Methodist University in 1956, where she was inducted into Phi Beta Kappa. After graduation she told her mother who was a teacher that she had decided to go into law. A mother of a classmate who was a professor of law at Baylor, who was one of only three women teaching law in accredited schools in 1950, had encouraged her to go for law. She thought she was lucky, but those who knew her felt she deserved to be recommended by the dean of admissions at S.M.U. law school to be awarded a full scholarship to attend the University of Chicago Law School. She says, "I loved everything about the ideals of justice, fairness, and dignity that I studied there." She decided to teach law and to devote her life's work to law reform. She served as book review editor of the *Chicago Law Review*.

She obtained a clerkship with Justice Roger Traynor of the California Supreme Court. Herma tells a story of how difficult it was to wear the proper clothes and interview when she was recommended for a faculty spot at Boalt Hall the Law School of U.C. Berkeley. Those were the days when well-dressed women wore hats and gloves. Her problem was with choosing the proper hat. Herma was chosen to fill an available faculty seat and became one of that small group of women who became law professors. In spite of her sex she came to be a Fellow of the Academy of Arts and Sciences, a member of the American Philosophical Society, and made a member of the Council and

Executive Committee of the American Law Institute. She is past president of both the Association of American Law schools and the Order of the Coif. She was admitted to the bars of the State of California and the United States Supreme Court. The list goes on and on to her becoming the dean of the Boalt School of Law at the University of California, the first woman to hold that high office. The important thing to me is what she accomplished during those eventful steps forward.

Her writings in books and papers were effective in helping the role of women in our society advance on the long road to equality with men and for a woman's right to choose. She taught Laws on Marriage, Family Law, California Marital Property, Sex-Based Discrimination, and Conflict of Laws. Here she was a true hero. With her position and stature, she was in a place where she could command a large audience of legal professionals and lay people.

I had the privilege of consulting on some of the medical references in a book she wrote with Ruth Bader Ginsburg. She is working on a history of women law professors in the United States between 1900 and 2000.

With all the books she has written especially on Sex-based Discrimination and all the papers and all the talks, she has been an honored teacher to her students, and she is a hero to them and especially to women, and therefore to me.

Simon and Jeanette Kapstein

11.   SIMON KAPSTEIN

Simon Kapstein was my father. He was a hero for me and for many who had the good fortune to know him. When he was in his twenties as second in command of the E.P. Carlton Company he fired a store manager, his senior in age for harassing women employed in his store. The employees in the many stores he supervised were paid a living wage with equal pay for equal work. Such actions were unusual in the very first part of the twentieth century.

Simon was born in Kiev in 1866. As a baby he was taken with his parents to Fall River, Massachusetts where he grew up. When he graduated from high school, he looked for a job to replace his work delivering newspapers. He later wrote that he was intrigued by a store in Fall River that had a big red sign with gold letters; E.P. CHARLTON COMPANY 5 & 10-CENT STORE. He went in and talked with Mr. Charlton who hired him as a stock boy at three dollars a week. He persevered and enrolled in a local business school for a two-year evening course in management, as he said, surrounding himself with business periodicals pertaining to stock and floor work and merchandising. From then on promotions and raises followed; first as assistant to the receiving clerk, then to the clerk's job when that man was promoted to store manager. Then followed a variety of jobs in various aspects of company operations, including window trimming. After he had been with the company for three and a half years, Mr. Charlton asked him to go to San Francisco to reestablish the company there after the earthquake. He was only twenty. His parents felt that he was too young but the next year he went. He was on his way.

When I was growing up, I got to know most of this story, and I considered following my father's footsteps. Whenever I got a chance, I worked in one of his stores. I won a first prize in a window-decorating contest. I even managed a store when my father was on vacation.

Mr. Charlton never wanted Simon to return to the head office in Fall River. He was too valuable in the west. However, Simon was able to get home to Fall River to woo and marry Jeannette Bedrick in a major social event in February 1914. She had always been a favorite of his. By the standards of that time he was wealthy and she came from a good and successful family. He took his bride to Oakland California where he had just opened a store. She was depressed at first, being young in a strange place, but she and Simon met a couple also on their honeymoon, Dora and Harry Camp, who became lifelong friends. This team later together and separately became heroes when they settled in San Francisco.

The Kapstein's first child, Dorothy, was born in Oakland. The store in Oakland was a success; so Simon was sent to Portland to open a store there. I was born in Portland. My first memories in life are from there. My Dad was always thinking of things my sister and I might like. In my case my first experience with animals was with rabbits that I got to feed. Though my parents made lifelong friends in Portland, Simon prevailed on Mr. Carlton to let him move to San Francisco and to manage the store there at 5th and Market Street permanently. From there, he continued to be Mr. Charlton's West Coast supervisor. That store was successful and placed Simon in a good position.

Simon had a genius for making large profits on smart buys. As the United States got closer to war in

The E. P. Charlton 5 & 10 cent store on Washington Street in Portland, Oregon, (1905) was one of the first of Charlton's West Coast stores.

World War I an embargo was placed on purchases from Germany. At the time, a major supplier of toys to the United States was Germany. The wholesalers of toys felt that there would be no market. Simon bought for his store in San Francisco many toys, thousands of them for an average of around 18 cents. He put them on sale for around one dollar. He had to arrange for police protection of the store because of the mobs that wanted to buy these toys.   In addition, people once in the store often bought other merchandise or ate at the food counter. He sold all the toys.

Some time later, there was a major move with phonograph records moving from the large vinyl to the smaller long-play type. The wholesalers had huge

Interior of the Portland, Oregon store. Note the wooden floors and the imprinted "tin" ceiling.

inventories of the old records. Simon, knowing that large numbers of people still had their old phonographs, bought a huge supply of the old records for much less than a dollar and sold them for a dollar each. When Bobby Pins appeared, Simon appreciated their potential. He bought the patent and the producer. He gave this and the market for the pins to the Woolworth stores, and to his brothers who prospered until they overextended their business.   Years later when he formed the Kay Novelty Company, he noted Christmas decorations of foil butterflies at a florist on Grant Avenue, Podesta, and Baldocci. He liked them. He bought the patent and sold many thousands of them to his old firm, Woolworth.

In business school, Simon learned to use a typewriter. When I was entering high school, he encouraged me to learn, for which I am grateful. He wrote his regular reports to Mr. Charlton in an excellent fashion that encouraged Carleton to give Simon increasing responsibility. I will give you a sample. He wrote hundreds.

"I trust that you will agree with me that in letting Mr. Springman go, as I did, was to the best interest of the Company and protects us from cheap 'John Lawyer.' We have a force of help to be proud of; all are ladylike, courteous, and clean cut. It would not be to our advantage to make any change in help. After thinking it over, it would not be doing the young lady justice who refused to tie up with Mr. Springman. I further give her credit for doing so. She is a clean cut, honest little girl and of a nice family, and Mr. Springman was trying to take advantage of her. After going into several confidential chats with clerks of the store, I find that Mr. Springman tried to propose to several young ladies. If Mr. Springman was that weak to let drink upset him over a girl, I am sure that you or anyone else has no further use for him."

Though San Francisco was a fairly liberal city, anti-Semitism existed. No golf club would accept Jews. Simon and some friends decided they would form a golf club where Jews and Gentiles would be welcome. The product of that was the formation of the Lake Merced Golf Club in 1922 that has not discriminated except against those who were not good citizens. This Golf Club was one of the first of its kind in the country. The founders are heroes to generations of golfers.

In early 1912, the E.P. Charlton Co. merged with the F.W. Woolworth Co. with the agreement that all employees be retained in grade. Such was certainly the case with Simon who received the following letter. "You have been a valuable asset and there will always be a good position for you as the firm exists or its successors, E.P. Charlton."

But there was a sinister factor in play—intolerance within the Woolworth organization. Simon Kapstein was Jewish and the F.W. Woolworth Co. did not have any employees of the Jewish faith in senior supervisory levels. Charlton did not discriminate, hiring his personnel for their work ethic and productivity, not by race or religion. He had insisted that Woolworth hire all of his employees at levels they held at the time of the merger.

Simon persevered and managed all the stores on the West Coast. Because of continued pressure, he asked for and got the position of manager of the Woolworth store at 5th and Market Streets in San Francisco. At that time the manager got in addition to his salary a percentage of the profits. The store became the most successful Woolworth store in the country. Soon Simon's income was greater than that of anyone else except top executives. In 1930, the president of the Woolworth Company came to San Francisco to inspect the store. He decided they did not want a Jew to manage the largest (and most profitable) store in the United States. Simon had enough. He resigned though he remained a good friend of many of his old colleagues at Woolworth.

At this point, Simon decided to move back to Boston to see how it would be living close to his family and to Jeannette's. He sold all his securities except Woolworth (before the crash). We moved to Chestnut Hill outside of Boston. That involved taking our seven passenger Cadillac, our cook, and all of us on a ship through the Panama Canal and Cuba. We had a beautiful home with lots of land. We even acquired a dog that we loved. I went to the Boston Latin School (which was a life-changing experience) and my sister went to Choate.

After we were there less than two years, the crash of '29 occurred. My father and mother both had huge families. Almost all of the members lost all or most of their assets, even my father's brothers whom Simon had set up in business. Simon bailed them all out. He was a family hero. He decided he would have to make another fortune. He became a hero to me and to many others in doing so. He decided the place to do that was San Francisco.

It took him a while to decide he should form a chain of stores, Standard Five and Ten Cent Stores. That was a tough time to start a new business, as the recession that followed the crash of 1929 was severe. I began working in the main store on Polk St. after school. My young brother made packages of foreign stamps to sell in the store, and my mother tried and found that she was an excellent salesperson, but she thought she could contribute more.

Jeannette Kapstein, after trying a few sales projects, decided to become an interior designer. She did a sort of internship working with Carl Leingfelt in his large building. From there she developed an exceedingly successful practice. She became a hero to a generation of young couples who married after World War II. She showed them and their parents how to improve on what had been a rather boring style of furnishing homes and hotels prior to the war. Included in her clients were the Saint Francis and the Fairmont hotels. She became the president of the local A.I.D. and even got to talk with Jackie Kennedy when Jackie was redecorating the White House. She also became a hero to the residents of Laguna Honda, a public old age home in San Francisco, where she went once a week to play the piano and sing with residents there. She was a hero to that group of her colleagues who suffered in the AIDS epidemic. She visited them, brought them food, and joined them in their last efforts to have parties.

Simon was proud of the fact that he "came back." He was a hero to those who worked for him. He always paid good wages. His sales people earned better salaries than those in similar positions in the major stores "downtown." He always paid equal pay for equal work. He had the wonderful ability to be friendly with people in all walks of life from local peddlers to Governor Brown.

After the War, he was joined by my brother, Robert, who had gone to Harvard Business School while in the navy and to Stanford Business School after

Jeannette Kapstein

the War. This added a new dimension to the business that expanded more. They developed a total of ten stores (seven Standard and three Shaw/Kerner}. The stores, especially that on California Street, made an effort to obtain things they did not have for people who were good customers. That resulted in unusually loyal clientele. Simon and Robert were good and honored citizens for hiring, if at all possible, neighbors' children who needed a job. Among the first was Guenther Leopold who worked his way up *à la* Kapstein to now being owner of the company.

Simon with his partner Robert had new freedom. He gave up golf, formed a fishing group of diverse men who had a wonderful time together. He was now able to travel extensively making friends everywhere.

I would like to tell you about one experience with my Dad in Venice. He had brought our whole family to the Gritti to celebrate my parents' 50th

Simon Kapstein

wedding anniversary. At breakfast with him one day, I asked him what his plans for the day were. He said that it was his day to bring wine to the gondoliers. He asked if I wanted to come. Of course, I did. We then got a large gondola and loaded it with barrels of wine. In Venice on the Grand Canal there were places along the canal where you hired a gondola to take you across. At each of these he left a small barrel of wine on each side. As we made our way down the Grand Canal there were shouts from both sides, "Kappy, Kappy!"

Simon also formed a successful business called Kay Novelties. "The ironic part of this was that the Woolworth stores on the West Coast became his best customers."

After a long and productive life of eighty-five years he felt that he had succeeded twice. I know he never thought of himself as a hero. Many did.

Nancy Pelosi

12.   NANCY PELOSI

I first met Nancy Pelosi the day after I received the French Legion of Honor from French president Sarkozy. She came over that day to congratulate me by name in the Capitol where the French president was to speak. She was already a hero to most San Franciscans when she led the action to make the Presidio in San Francisco a national park instead of a massive real estate project. Recently, she became a national hero when she led the drive to pass the Affordable Care Act ("Obamacare").

To me, it is interesting to know how this woman was able to get to a position where she was able to do these wonderful things.

Pelosi was born in Baltimore, the youngest of six children. Her Dad was a Democratic U.S. Congressman from Maryland, Thomas D'Alesandro, Jr. and mayor of Baltimore from 1967 to 1971. Her brother, Tomas, was also Mayor of Baltimore. He too was a Democrat. Naturally, she got involved in politics at an early age. After she graduated from Trinity College with a B.A. in political science she interned for Senator Daniel Brewster, (Democrat from Maryland).

She met Paul Pelosi when she was in college in San Francisco. They were married in Baltimore in

1963. They moved first to New York then to San Francisco where Paul's brother Ronald was a member of the Board of Supervisors. Paul has been a major supporter and in my mind they make a perfect team. In San Francisco, deep into Democratic politics, she met Congressman Philip Burton who was respected in Democratic circles. He recognized Nancy's potential in politics and as a legislator. She had an unusual grasp of each. He was a great help in moving her along. In l976 she was elected to the Democratic National Committee. Then came a long series of important positions in the party. Phil Burton died in 1963 and his wife inherited his position. When she developed cancer, she gave up her post and picked Nancy to take her place and promised maximum support. Nancy Pelosi won a close election. She has won since then and, of course, is Congressman from San Francisco.

With all these activities, she has still been able to have and raise five children and seventeen grandchildren. Her daughter, Christine, is already well positioned in the Democratic Party.

In 2001 she was elected Minority Whip. On January 3, 2006, she was elected Speaker of the House, the first woman to hold that office and to hold the highest rank in our country for a woman in U.S. history. She became a hero in many ways more:

She opposed President Bush's attempt to privatize part of social security and won.

She blocked impeachment proceedings against President Bush.

She opposed Bush's "Troop Surge" in Iraq, feeling that the problems there could not be solved militarily.

She was a vital player in helping to pass Health Care Reform.

She criticized the People's Republic of China for its handling of Tibet.

She was against the Partial Birth Abortion Act of 2003.

She voted in favor of lifting the ban on privately funded abortions.

She is in favor background checks for gun owners and the banning of assault weapons.

Socially, she is relaxed and a good listener. In talking with her, you might easily wonder whether she is the woman who is one of the most powerful politicians in America.

She continues to be a hero to me as she works to preserve the liberal point of view.

Jerry Brown

13.   JERRY BROWN

Jerry Brown became a hero for me when he helped me and all the doctors in California to get great improvement in their malpractice insurance.

In 1975, I was elected chief of staff at the Mount Zion Medical Center. Almost immediately I was faced with problem of the rising cost of malpractice insurance. I wrote the following to the *San Francisco Chronicle*, which published it.

A SOLUTION IS NEEDED

Editor: I am appalled by the apparent lack of interest shown by the news media in the problem of malpractice insurance for doctors. The average physician doing a surgical specialty is faced with a tremendous rise in premiums. In my office of three physicians the premiums will rise from approximately $13,000 per year to approximately $55,000 per year. This outrageously high charge will cause a number of problems. Many physicians will be unable to meet the premiums, since they will not be able to raise fees enough to cover the costs. The patients who pay

doctors will be faced with markedly
increased fees, which their insurance
carriers are unlikely to fund at this time.

"Faced with this problem, many
physicians are choosing to leave practice
until some equitable solution has been
worked out. This may well result in the
closure of some hospital facilities for all but
acute care. Certainly, the public will suffer.

"There must be a public demand for
legislative correction of this situation.

JOHN A. KERNER, M.D.
San Francisco

On April 30, 1975, 250 anesthesiologists in 50
Bay Area medical centers went on strike and would
only give anesthesia for emergencies, not normal
childbirth. Many other doctors joined them by not
hospitalizing patients except for emergencies. This was
a disaster for the hospitals. The margin of profit usually
came from elective surgery. They all began to bleed
dollars. The medical societies appealed for help from
the state but nothing seemed to happen. There were
no laws in California concerning malpractice
insurance.

The whole problem was covered in national
newspapers and on television. Because of my letter and
my position my name was often brought up. Then
came a surprising event.

My wife and I were playing golf on a Sunday. A
man from the pro shop same out to tell me that they

had received a phone call from Governor Jerry Brown who wanted to talk with me. I called the number he had left. I was told to come to the State Building as soon as possible. I left the golf club at once, stopped by my office to pick up material I had been working on, left off my wife and headed for the California State Building in our Civic Center. At the door, I was greeted by a police officer who informed me that the Governor was waiting for me in the conference room. I was escorted there.

The conference room was impressive. What really impressed me though was that Governor Brown was there with what looked like his entire staff including the insurance commissioner and an assemblyman. The most surprising thing about those present was that there were no other doctors—not the president of the medical society of California or San Francisco.

Governor Brown asked me what I thought he should do about the strike. It was important that something be done quickly, because important medical care was being denied if it was not classified as "emergency." So I said that the governor should make a strong public statement stating what he proposed to do and that such a statement might induce the anesthesiologists to call off their strike. He asked what he should say in his statement.

I suggested that there be a $250,000 limit on judgments for "pain and suffering" and that premiums be rolled back because of that. Also, there should be a shorter time limit for the filing of malpractice claims. After each of my suggestions, Brown spoke into a phone on his desk (which I later found was connected to someone from the trial lawyers group). He would say, "The doctor here says..." He did not tell me the response.

After the governor left the room, members of his cabinet quizzed me for over an hour. I stressed the importance of something being done at the state level, since medical care was in turmoil. The hospitals were in increasing financial difficulties. I also gave the secretary a list of suggestions that I had been working on with others.

After a terrible month for hospitals, I got a call from the Governor's secretary that he had asked Alister McAlister who had been present at our meeting, to present my suggestions to the State Legislature and that they had all been passed. California has had the best malpractice laws in the country. Jerry Brown was a hero for getting this done in spite of the trial lawyers.

At the time I met Jerry Brown he was one of the youngest governors in the history of our state. He has had an interesting life and from my point of view he has been a hero for the causes he has supported and for his actions as a politician.

Edmund "Jerry" Brown Jr. was born in San Francisco on April 7,1938. His father "Pat" Brown" was Governor of California. Jerry was his only son. He went to Santa Clara University for a year. He studied to be a priest for three years, but left that to go to U.C. Berkeley. He then went to Yale Law School. Next he was selected to be a law clerk for California Supreme Court Justice Matthew Tobriner who was highly respected. Brown followed all that with a long political career.

In a field of 124, he placed first in a selection for the Los Angeles Community College Board of Trustees. He was elected as Secretary of State in California in 1971. He argued before the California Supreme Court and became a hero to many of us when he won cases against Standard Oil, T & T International, Gulf Oil, and Mobil for election law violations. He drafted the California Political Reform Act.

In his first term as governor in 1975, he again was a hero to many of us when he championed the following goals:

He was a strong advocate against the death penalty. He had a intense interest in environmental issues. He was interested in keeping expenses down— he lived in a modest apartment instead of the governor's mansion. He drove a Plymouth, rather than being driven in the governor's limousine. The state had a budget surplus of $5 billion in spite of proposition 13 which had cut taxes.

He tried three times for the Presidential nomination but failed.

In 1999 he became mayor of Oakland. There he found the city in a severe economic downturn and loosing residents. He immediately began programs that would help. He got the Fox Theater refurbished; Jack London Square restored, and especially began the revitalizing of the Port of Oakland. He was able to begin the resurgence of the downtown. He established a program to provide low-cost housing. All of these moves produced an increase in the population of

10,000. The Port of Oakland is now one of the most active in the country. Jerry Brown became a hero to many in Oakland and the State of California.

In 2007 Brown was elected Attorney General of California. In that position he could again bring up his fight against capital punishment which made him a hero again to me. In 2008 he filed a fraud lawsuit against Countrywide Financial's practice of getting homeowners to buy risky mortgages. He was one of the first to take this kind of action and he won up to $8.4 billion. He also helped overturn Proposition 8 that was against same-sex marriage, a hero again.

He became governor for a third time in 2011. He has already moved the state to a much better position than the former governor had left it. It now looks as though the state will make progress in better support for education, the generation of jobs, and combatting the effects of a long drought. I predict that we will have occasions to again toast him as a hero.

14.   HERB CAEN

Herb Caen was a hero to me and to most San Franciscans. I did not get to know him until he was already established in San Francisco. However, I, like most San Franciscans, read his column daily starting shortly after his arriving in our city in 1936. Though he often was called "Mr. San Francisco," I preferred "Boswell by the Bay." Though I enjoyed his columns for their gossip, one liners, insider news, and his three-dot style, I respected him for feeling as I did that the war in Vietnam was a major mistake. At that point he became a hero to me.

I got to know Herb when I cared for two of his four wives. Whenever he came to my office or when I met him on the street, he was always well dressed in an elegant style in a suit and fedora. He continued this style of an era I always respected.   In spite of the fact that he coined the word "beatnik," he did not succumb to the growing informal type dress and neither have I. When I go to any nice event, I wear a jacket and usually a tie. I follow Herb in that.

Herb's columns of "local going-on, insider gossip, political and social happenings, painful puns and offbeat anecdotes" were only a part of his love for San Francisco, its people and atmosphere.

HERB CAEN

Merry Christmas, Everybody!

AH YES, and happy Hanukkah, too.
To Johnny Goy and Fung Kuen Jew,
Chief Tony Ribera and Doreen Foo,
Shirley Black and Vida Blue,
The koala bears at the S.F. Zoo,
Giraudo (Lou) and Bierman (Sue)
Plus a nip of the foggy foggy dew
For you and you and I do mean you! (Whew).

SEASON'S greetings, clear as a bell,
To Frank 'n' Wendy, Charlotte and Mel,
Ronnie Schell and Holman Monell,
And the theme from the opera "William Tell,"
For Courtney (Del) and Ronnie Mobell;
Too late for shopping now so a check'll
Go to the symphony's Nancy Bechtle,
Bradford Kopp and Larry Capelli,
Darius Aidala, Ken Malucelli,
Carole Hays and Matthew Kelly,
Sandy Walker, Melvin Belly,
Walter Fong and Erdman (Helly).

COMES it now a Yuletide carol,
For Robert Cromey and Forman (Darryl),
Harry de Wildt and slick Willie Brown,
Jack Molinari and Bozo the Clown,
Carlos Santana, Joe Montana,
Marianna Banana and Mark Fontana,
Joseph J. O'Donohue Four,
(A dandy fellow, *jamais un bore*),
And let us give some Toys for Tots
To the Ronnie Lotts and Gustavo Satts,
Nini Martin, Harris Barton,
Dolly Parton and the great Mae Sarton
(who?).

NOTHING, puhleeze, as schlock as a wok
For Big Jim Schock and Winston Kock,
Or Grover Sales and the Prentis Hales,
The Georgie Bushes, the Danny Quayles;
Meanwhile a beer for Bill and Hillary,
Tipper and Al plus the heavy artillery,
And no, that is not the rhyme of the year,
So Norman Lear, meet Jake McNear;
Tidings now of comfort and joy
To Kenneth Maley and Tommy Toy,
David Pratt and C. Bland Platt,
Barry Bonds and his big brown bat.

THE CHOIR will please sing a capella
For Cap'n Jack Newlin and Ben Langella,
Joe DiMaggio, Ryann Abeel,
Proctor Jones and Carolyn Piel,
Scott McKellar, Jeffrey Heller,
Otto Teller and Merla Zeller-
Bach, with lovable Frederick Goerner,
Tom "Sport" Rooney and Doc John Kerner,
Perry Butler, Baby Jo Schuman,
Ellen vos and Walter Newman

San Francisco Chronicle

HERB CAEN

That's Me All Over

THE FEE ENTERPRISE system: In medical terms, you'd have to say Presbyterian Hospital is in serious if not critical shape — a $17 million debt and low occupancy, but incredibly good research and surgical facilities in its fortress-like new building on Buchanan. Meanwhile, famed Mt. Zion, which was losing $100,000 a month a year ago, is now well in the black, thanks to the efforts of such as Rhoda (Mrs. Richard) Goldman and Dr. John Kerner, the energetic Chief of Staff ... This is what has led to rumors of a merger of the two facilities, a possibility that, say insiders, "is still far in the future but being discussed. San Francisco's problem is not unique — too many hospitals, too many overlapping research programs and no control."

★ ★ ★

Herb was born Herbert Eugene Caen on April 3, 1916 and died February 2, 1997 of lung cancer. Almost every citizen who lived in San Francisco after 1936, when he came to town, remembers him. I agree that the secret of Herb's success was "his outstanding ability to take a wisp of fog, a chance phrase overheard in an elevator, a happy child on a cable car, a deb in a dizzy over a social reversal, a family in distress and give each circumstance the magic touch that makes a reader an understanding eyewitness of the day's happenings."

With that he added much of the tone of his idol, Walter Winchell, that he used with three dots between items most of which were short.

A special Pulitzer Prize called him the "voice and conscience of San Francisco." Herb wondered about that, since he felt that Pulitzers usual went to deep thinkers.

Herb Caen

Herb was born in Sacramento and often clued himself "the Sacramento kid." On occasion, he would point out that his parents, Lucien Caen, a pool hall operator, and his mother, Augusta Caen, had spent a summer in San Francisco. In high school he wrote a column, "Corridor Gossip" and covered sports for the Sacramento Union.

When he first came to San Francisco in 1936, he began writing a radio column for the *San Francisco Chronicle*. When that column was discontinued, in 1938, he proposed a daily column "It's News to Me." However, World War II came along. He served in the Air Force. After the war he worked on the *San Francisco Chronicle* where the column was simply "Herb

Caen." The column had Herb Caen over a San Francisco skyline with the Trans America Pyramid "flaccid" six days a week. He worked for the *Chronicle*, except for a brief stint on the *San Francisco Examiner*, for the rest of his life. "What makes him unique," a colleague wrote in 1996, "is that on good days his column offers everything you expect from an entire newspaper—in just 25 or so items, 1,000 or so words." Readers who turned to Herb on Feb 14,1966, learned that: "Willie Mays' home was on the market for $110,000. The Bank of America now owned the block where it wanted to build its headquarters. 'Dr. Zhivago' director David Lean was in town. Mike Connolly was ready to concede that the situation in Vietnam was complex: "Even my cab driver can come up with a solution."

We all tended to try to use words he coined or made popular: "beatnik," "hippie," "Berserkeley."

Herb was very careful to be sure his quotes were correct, if someone told him something and he did not want his name mentioned, Herb would often write, "Strange de Jim says." I know a young woman when asked if she went to Stanford. She replied, I slept with a lot of men from Stanford. Does that qualify? Herb printed that without mentioning her name.

Here are a few quotes:

"The only thing wrong with immortality is that it tends to go on forever"

"Isn't it nice that people who prefer Los Angeles to San Francisco live there?"

"The trouble with born again Christians is that they are even bigger pain the second time around."

"A man begins cutting his wisdom teeth the first time he bites off more than he can chew."

"The number of foggy days over the city is never reported, reportedly. But take it from me—there's enough to satisfy everyone, and dissatisfy somebody."

June 14, 1996 was officially celebrated in San Francisco as Herb Caen Day. There was a motorcade and parade ending at the Ferry Building where a "pantheon of movers, shakers, celebrities, and historical figures including Walter Cronkite spoke." When Herb was told San Francisco mayors were at liberty to attend, Herb quipped, "Obviously the Grand Jury hasn't been doing its job." In his honor there is a walk along the Embarcadero christened "Herb Caen Way."

Herb was again my hero and that of many others when he repeatedly advocated the destruction of a freeway that had been built along the Embarcadero. He called it "The Dambarcadero."

In one of his last columns he wrote: "If I go to heaven, I'm going to do what every San Franciscan does who goes to heaven. He looks around and says, "It ain't bad but it ain't San Francisco."

15.   MARY JANE BRINTON

In my lifetime Mary Jane Brinton was a hero and much more. She helped make it possible for me to do a great deal for medical education. She enthusiastically helped me in my cancer research. Most important she became a dear friend.

I first met Mary Jane when she was in labor with her second child. Mary Jane had just moved to San Francisco with her husband Bill and her first child Bill Junior. She was a patient of my professor of Obstetrics and Gynecology, Herbert Traut. Doctor Traut was out of town to speak at a major meeting. He had signed out to Daniel Morton, a favorite professor of mine, and of my fellow residents at the University of California Medical School in San Francisco.

Mary Jane entered the U.C. Hospital in active labor. I was the resident on call. I checked Mrs. Brinton and called Doctor Morton who was at home not far away. He said he would be right over. Mary Jane's labor was moving rapidly; so, I moved her into a delivery room and gave her some analgesia with nitrous oxide and oxygen. When delivery became inevitable, I decided to deliver the baby and not try to hold it back until Doctor Morton arrived. The delivery went well. The baby a girl was in perfect health. I had made a small incision called an episiotomy and was just finishing the repair when Doctor Morton appeared. He was cool as always. Having found all was well he reported that to Mary Jane. I followed her in the hospital. She did well post delivery. When she left the hospital, she left a beautiful decanter as a gift for me with a nice note. About two years later, I had finished by residency training at U.C.S.F. and had established an office on Van Ness Avenue in San Francisco. One of my first patients was Mary Jane who was pregnant again. I had had no contact with her since the birth of her daughter. I asked her why she did not return to

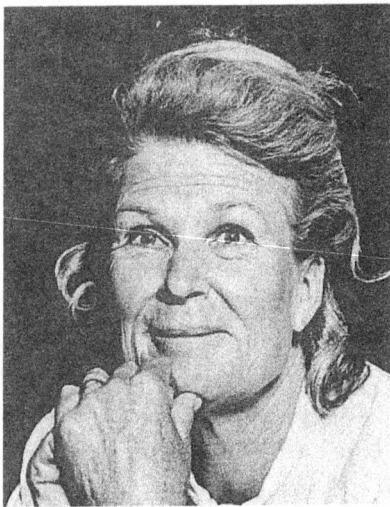

Mary Jane Brinton

Doctor Traut and she let me know that she felt more at ease with me. I reported all of this to Doctor Traut. I did not want to develop any hostility from my chief who also was the most influential physician in my specialty in San Francisco. Doctor Traut was gracious and wished me well.

Mary Jane's pregnancy went well and her delivery, like the last, was uncomplicated. I had learned that Mary Jane was a granddaughter of John Deere who had invented the steel plow and whose family now owned the Deere Tractor Company, a major provider of heavy farming equipment. So fortunately I could provide a private room in a new area with a sitting room for a private nurse. Shortly after Mary Jane and the baby went home, I got a call from the director of the hospital, Mount Zion. He said he had received a check from a fiduciary for $10,000, a large sum at that time. He thought it might have come from Bill Brinton so did I, but I was not sure. In any event, it increased my stature as the youngest member of the department.

When I first went into practice my professor and chairman of our department called me into his office to give me advice. One of the subjects he wanted to talk about was a practice of obstetricians in San Francisco. Obstetricians would ask their new patients how much their husbands earned and charged them accordingly. He thought that I should have one fee that might be lowered if necessary but not raised if I thought the husband was well off. Then he added the most important instruction. He said that some patients or their husbands might ask me why I did not charge them more. I should reply to them that I had a fund, the money from which would be used for medical education and research in my field. If the patient or her husband wanted to contribute to that, I would be happy, but I would not raise my fee. I had just established such a fund on the request of another patient mentioned in this book. Shortly after this delivery, my fund received a letter from a fiduciary in New York that my fund had received stock worth over $100,000. They did not and would not tell me where that came from, but I, of course, guessed. From then on I reported to Mary Jane what my fund was doing. Gifts

WILLIAM M. BRINTON
MARY JANE W. BRINTON

461

1-2/210/038

April 16, 19 87

PAY TO THE ORDER OF MOUNT ZION HOSPITAL

$ 75,000.00

* * * * SEVENTY-FIVE THOUSAND and 00/100* * * * * * DOLLARS

CHASE

The Chase Manhattan Bank, N.A.
Rockefeller Plaza at 49th Street
New York, N.Y. 10020

MEMO

⑆021000021⑆ 038 1 189000⑈ 0461

of that size and greater began coming yearly. They helped me to establish a residency program in obstetrics and gynecology at Mount Zion Hospital in San Francisco. The program was approved by the American Board and ended up as the only such program in a private hospital in San Francisco. The fund also made it possible for me to establish a research laboratory that has produced two promising anticancer drugs. After a couple of years, Mary Jane was aware that I had guessed where the money was coming from and she began sending checks.

When Mount Zion Hospital joined with the University of California Medical Center in San Francisco, Mary Jane wrote a check for one million dollars with which we established a section on Cancer

Genetics, one on Cancer Risk, and a ward for children with cancer. Mary Jane would not let me put her name on any of these, but I did put her mother's name on the children's ward.

During this time, I had the pleasure of delivering a third daughter for Mary Jane and Bill.

It is important for readers to know that during the many years I knew Mary Jane she did a great deal more then have and grow children and help John Kerner and his many projects.

First, you should know a bit more about this wonderful woman. She was born on December 3, 1921 in Chicago to Charles Deere Wiman and Patricia Southall Wiman that made here a great granddaughter of John Deere. She grew up in Moline Illinois. She went to Bennington College but did not quite finish her degree because of marriage. But years later she went back to school in San Francisco at Lone Mountain College where she finally got her bachelor's degree. She married Bill Brinton in 1943. They lived in Charlottesville, Virginia, until they moved to San Francisco in 1948 with their young son Bill. That is the year I had the good fortune to meet her.

Mary Jane was always interested in education. I recognized that with her interest in my residency-training program. In 1966 she helped gather a group of parents who founded the Urban School of San Francisco that continues to be successful. I have had the pleasure of lecturing there and meeting with the outstanding group of students mostly telling them about World War II. She established the Flanders Fellowship program at the U.C. Graduate School of

Education in honor of Professor Emeritus Ned Flanders. The fellowships are awarded to recruit, prepare, and sustain new teachers who are role models for disadvantaged youth in urban schools. To date, over 350 fellowships have been awarded. To that group she is a hero.

She established a wonderful idea for students at New Traditions Alternative Elementary School in San Francisco. She hosted what she called a "Wonder Desk" which was placed in a hallway once a week. Students would come to her desk with any question from history to sex. I often was interested in hearing some of the kids' questions.

In 1999 an article in the U.C. Berkeley Graduate School of Education newsletter had this to say, "A role model in her own right, (Mary Jane) Brinton is on a mission to revitalize urban education."

She became a hero again. She had always had a concern for high-need populations. She was especially concerned about their health and welfare. In 2001 she established the Brinton Psychiatric Homeless Project which provides psychiatric care and mental health services for those homeless persons in San Francisco who suffer from mental illness and have limited or no access to such services.

Her family owned a home in Santa Barbara, built I think by Mary Jane's grandfather. There, her gifts established Neighborhood Clinics providing low-cost bicultural and bilingual mental services to those in low-income neighborhoods. A hero again, Mary Jane was moved by the horror of Katrina and the oil spill near New Orleans. She sent her son and his wife to find opportunities to assist the community by improving health resources and job opportunities. From what she learned, Mary Jane set up a Family and Healing Clinic in partnership with Tulane University which opened in 2011. It provides primary care to low-income members of the community as well as hands-on experience for physicians and other healthcare workers in training.

Mary Jane was again my hero when she contributed to chairs in my name at the University of California Medical School in San Francisco. Karen Smith-McCune holds the first of these chairs. Karen is now a world authority on diseases of the uterine cervix. The second chair is a "distinguished" chair. That chair involved raising 2.5 million dollars. Mary Jane helped greatly in reaching that goal. John Chan who raised the U.C. women's anticancer group to national importance held it. I wanted to put her name on the last chair and she insisted that it have my name. That was the way Mary Jane was.

She and Bill had interest in public affairs. She was generous in her support of the League of Women Voters and the Center for Investigative Reporting (CIR). In 2002, the CIR honored her with their Donor of the Year award. For at least thirteen years she worked on homeless policy issues with her friend, Sister Bernie of the Religious Witness with the Homeless.

She loved animals and refused to give any money to me or other researchers who used animals in their research—even mice. Accordingly, my lab became wonderfully expert in the use of tissue cultures.

She loved dogs and over the years had many, usually two at a time. She had a statue of a favorite. Horses, too, were a "passion" for her and she rode for many years. She finally gave up after being thrown many times, the last being from her daughter Delia's horse that she was riding bareback in Golden Gate Park. In her later years she became a hero to a large flock of parrots. Their home had been on Telegraph Hill and in that area. They moved to the edge of the Presidio when building disrupted their home. Mary Jane thought they would be happier in her rebuilt garden that already attracted birds especially humming birds. She found what kind of food parrots liked and set up feeders. The parrots moved in. When pigeons found out there was food in Mary Jane's garden they came in large numbers stealing from the other birds. Mary Jane solved this problem by regular feeding of the pigeons in front of her house with food they liked. At the proper time of day when Mary Jane walked out her front door, the pigeons would swarm around her and she would feed them on the opposite side of the house from the parrots. The birds seemed to be happy with that arrangement.

Her generosity to family and friends, and to various teaching institutions seemed limitless. She became knowledgeable about degenerative mental disease and tried valiantly to overcome them when her beloved husband, Bill, became a victim.

She was a hero to all living things. Unfortunately she lost her life to cancer that she fought with others and me. She inspired me to continue the fight.

16.   GERSON BAKAR

Gerson Bakar is a hero to most of us San Franciscans for the major things he has helped develop such as the Mission Bay Campus of the University of California Medical School, the Jewish Community Center, Levi's Plaza, the Museum of Modern Art, and first-rate housing. From my way of thinking, one of the best things he has done is to marry Barbara Bass. In doing that he formed a formidable team that has done wonders that we will explore.

Gerson likes to talk about how he grew up on a chicken ranch in Petaluma, California. He went to college at the University of California Berkeley and graduated there in 1948. Since then, he has maintained an interest in all aspects of that school and has proved to be able to support many of its goals. After he graduated, his uncle, Max Bakar, encouraged him to go into building and helped Gerson to get started. Gerson first built two homes. Though they were not particularly successful financially, they created an interest in real estate that accelerated during the expansion of the Bay Area after World War II. He developed at least 20,000 family dwelling units from homes to apartments. He met and liked Wally Haas who led Levi Straus Co. That led among other things, to the development of Levi's Plaza that I consider one of the most beautiful districts in San Francisco with its magnificent landscaping including trees, splendid fountains and buildings. He developed other business buildings in the Bay Area always with an eye for quality.

After World War II there was a rush to build new housing for retuning veterans and business people. Gerson's buildings were of the highest quality as

Gerson Bakar

opposed to some others that were fragile, held up poorly, and were not particularly attractive.

He became co-chairman of the San Francisco Museum of Modern Art. He and Barbara had built a beautiful bridge to the roof of that building where they established a "world Class" roof garden with outstanding sculptures. Now Gerson has led the way to expanding that Museum to accommodate the Fisher Collection of Modern Art, one of the outstanding collections in the world.

Gerson provided major help and leadership in developing Menorah Park, an assisted living community in the center of San Francisco.

Gerson is an eminently decent man, informal, highly respected. He has the unusual ability to get things done in committees or on his own. He and Barbara as a team have the knowledge to choose important places to use their energy, and when they do they are unstinting in their efforts to make those projects succeed.

Gerson continues to set an example for civic minded people and in doing so he is a community hero.

Frank McCormick

17. FRANK McCORMICK

Frank McCormick was a hero to most of us at the U.C.S.F. Medical Center and to the community at large. He led the cancer program at U.C.S.F. from relative obscurity to national and international prominence.

After I completed my tour as chief of staff at the Mount Zion Medical Center in San Francisco, the institution had increasing financial difficulties in part because of the huge costs of the emergency room required by the City of San Francisco. The major supporters of the hospital did not wish to continue their support, so the decision was made to become a part of the University of California Medical Center. As soon as that move was decided upon, U.C.S.F. leaders ruled that the intensive care nursery at Mount Zion should be moved to the U.C. campus. I had developed that nursery while I was chief of obstetrics and gynecology and chief of staff at Mount Zion. It was a major moneymaker and superior to that at U.C.S.F. I suggested that some major project be moved to Mount Zion, since the Department of Obstetrics would have to close without the nursery.

Orthopedics was suggested and cancer. I thought that cancer would be a better option because I had sponsored a laboratory doing cancer research and

I had even explored building a cancer research building successfully. U.C.S.F. did not have a cancer center. Cancer care was divided amongst the various departments. The decision was made to have a cancer center on the Mount Zion Campus.

A major building was planned for cancer research and another for patient care. This was the first major project at U.C.S.F. since a new hospital was built shortly after World War II. Frank McCormick was chosen to lead the entire cancer program.

Frank had been educated at the University of Birmingham. England, B.Sc. 1972 in Biochemistry, University of Cambridge, England, Ph.D., 1975 in Biochemistry. He did a Post Doctoral Fellowship at Stony Brook, and another at the Imperial Cancer Research Fund in London. He became vice president of research of the Chiron Corporation. In 1992, he formed the company Onyx Corporation that became hugely successful. He was especially proud to have been chosen to be a Fellow of the Royal Society. With all that he appeared on the scene at U.C.S.F. in 1997. He immediately began to assemble a remarkable group of researchers and clinicians. I was pleased to be able to contribute from my fund a million dollars to establish a cancer genetics program and a cancer risk program. He brought over from Great Britain two former colleagues to establish research laboratories, Gerard Evan and Alan Balmain, and he set up his own laboratory. He included in his organization Karen Smith McCune who had a chair in gynecologic oncology that bears my name and later John Chan who holds a distinguished chair in the same field that also holds my name. The breast cancer program has been extremely successful led by Laura Esserman, as has the prostate cancer program led by Peter Carroll. The group that deals with malignant diseases of the blood is first rate. Frank seems to be aware of what is going on with cancer care and treatment in every department of the U.C.S.F. Medical Center. With his vast knowledge, he has been able to help strengthen the departments often, helping with funding. When he chairs a meeting he seems unusually familiar with any subject that is brought forward. I just do not know how he does that.

Frank's research is focused on signal transduction pathways in cancer cells. The group I sponsored has worked to utilize that knowledge with significant success. The lead drug we developed is now seeking funding for phase 3 trials. Our company is TriAct Therapeutics. His laboratory has also done extensive work on viruses that kill cancer cells selectively.

As a major hobby, Franks drives in auto racing with his Pro Formula Mazda. I keep telling him to drive carefully though he is well known for his driving skills. On weekends he drives at Infineon Raceway in Sonoma and Thunder Hill in Willows California. He says, "Racing is competitive and requires focus and dedication, and science does, too." Though he drives around 140 miles per hour, he says he doesn't find that especially fearsome and it gives him an "adrenalin rush that lasts for days." He says, "Giving a talk to a huge audience can be scarier." I wonder about that statement because he often is called upon to face large audiences like the American Association for Cancer Research where at a meeting in Washington there were 17,000 people registered and I am told he handled that in a "cool" way. His U.C.S.F. colleague, Martin McMahon, described a memorable dash across town in Frank's Mercedes, "You so much as tapped the gas and the thing took off like a rocket ship."

Recently, Frank moved his office from a small one in the cancer research building on the U.C.S.F.-Mount Zion campus to the new building at Mission Bay. There he has a beautiful corner office with windows on all sides with great views. I have never seen an office so neat. That is the way Frank does things. When Frank first arrived to take over, I was so impressed that I advised my brother to invest with me in Onyx. It was probably the best investment we ever made.

Frank and I agree that "staying in shape" is important not only in driving racing cars but also to be effective in the life work you choose. He has been a huge success in academia, private industry, and to a degree in racing. He says, while denying being hyper competitive, "Everyone wants to discover something big, nobody likes to be beaten or wrong or off the pace." He is handsome, gracious, and modest, so he will be missed as the Director of the U.C.S.F. Cancer program from which he has recently retired. I am sure we wear a great deal more from this heroic man.

18. LLOYD H. "HOLLY" SMITH Jr., M.D.

The University of California Medical School has been a major factor in my life. In the early sixties the school was loosing stature. To my mind that was all changed by Charles Wilson, Julius H. Comroe, and another hero of mine, Dr. Lloyd Hollingsworth Smith. Known to his friends and colleagues to this day as "Holly." The result of their work is that our medical school is considered one of the top in the U.S. and the world. Let's talk about "Holly."

When he came to U.C.S.F. in 1964, the school was celebrating its 100th anniversary as the oldest medical school west of the Mississippi. He found the school as he said: "With poor leadership, missed opportunities, lack of standards, and complacency."

However he recognized that the University of California was a great institution. Having had considerable association with Harvard he felt that the medical school could be raised to that level.

He came as chair of the Department of Medicine, which was then far below what would be expected from a great university. There was only one member of the Association of American Physicians. Holly made that two. They had few research grants even though the department had some fifty members. Under Holly that all changed. The department now has 550 or so members and receives more grants than almost any other department in the country. He is a hero to me and all who know what he has done for our school. How did that happen?

Holly grew up during the Depression in a small town in South Carolina. His father was a lawyer, but he had an uncle who had attended Johns Hopkins

"Holly" Smith Jr.

Medical School who had a great influence on him. His uncle was one of those who developed the yellow fever vaccine.

Holly went to Washington and Lee University. He entered Harvard Medical School at the age of 19. Important in his development was that after graduation he spent a year doing a fellowship in the Department of Physiology in which he worked developing the artificial kidney. He did his residency at Massachusetts General.

During the Korean War, he was sent to Walter Reed Army Institute of Research. There they studied viral hepatitis and diseases of the kidney. Then, he was sent to Korea to study problems in the care of wounded. Interestingly, he got permission to use an artificial kidney there since so many died from kidney failure. He then planned to prepare for a career in academic medicine. He did this with DeWitt Stetten Jr. in New York City, and the Karolinska Institute in Stockholm. While working in New York he married and likes to call the result a "biomass" of 6 children, and 17 grandchildren.

He then became chief medical resident after spending six months with Robert Loeb at Columbia. He was appointed chief of the endocrine unit at MGH. He spent a sabbatical year at Oxford (1963-1964) in the department of Sir Hans Krebs. While there he was asked to be a candidate for the chairmanship of the Department of Medicine at U.C.S.F. At that time he was about 40. I know of no one better prepared to be a chairman than perhaps my professor Herbert Traut.

The job he then did made him a hero for sure. He immediately wanted to help find better leadership for the campus. He found two men who would help greatly in this effort: The new chair of the Department of Surgery, J. Engelburt Dunphy, who had been his professor at Harvard, and to my mind most important, Julius Comroe, director of the Cardiovascular Research Institute.

These three raised the demands that knowledge of physiology was essential for all members of the faculty. For my department they brought in Robert Jaffe and "his Michigan mafia."

Like Herb Caen he is often quoted as follows:

—"Dress British, think Yiddish."
—"Plan ahead. Always be concerned about the danger of mural dyslexia, the inability to read handwriting on the wall."
—"Rather than wring our hands it would seem more sensible to find out whose hand to wring."

He says he picked these up over the years, but there are so many quotes I am quite sure many are entirely his.

He wrote a huge number of respected papers. He advised many important people and institutions. However to me, he still stands there tall, well dressed, reminding all of us who are involved in medical education that we must ourselves continue to be educated. For that alone, he is a hero.

19.   FRANK WORTHINGTON LYNCH, M.D.

I first met Doctor Lynch when I was a senior medical student. He changed my life and was my first medical hero.

At the first meeting of my senior class at the University of California Medical School in 1943, the dean asked for members of the class who might want to volunteer as interns while being responsible for most of their senior work. There was a shortage because of preparation for war. I was the only one to want to accept that challenge. One of my first assignments was in the Department of Obstetrics and Gynecology as acting intern. I had just completed working as an acting intern in general surgery.

The chairman of the Department of Obstetrics and Gynecology was Frank Lynch. To my surprise, I was told that one of my duties would be to go each night to the room where Doctor Lynch was trying to recover from one of a series of heart attacks. I was to listen to whatever he wanted to talk about and when he was ready to go to sleep, I was to give him an I.V. shot of barbiturate. I found that he only wanted doctors from his department to care for him. He did not trust the internists. He also had in a drawer next to his bed all sorts of medicines which he could take if he wanted.

During my six weeks on the service I got to know Doctor Lynch fairly well.

First I would like to tell you why he was a hero. The medical school of the University of California is now 150 years old. At the turn of the century men who had some training in that field taught obstetrics but gynecology was done by general surgeons and in part by general practitioners.

Gynecology was not recognized in most areas as a separate specialty. At Johns Hopkins Medical School, Obstetrics and Gynecology were two separate programs with organized training in each. In 1915, the leaders in the medical school felt that it was important to have formal training program in obstetrics and one in gynecology. When after a long search they decided to offer the position to Frank Lynch. He had convinced the search committee that the new department should be one called Obstetrics and Gynecology. In forming his faculty, two of his first appointees were women (unusual at that time), Alice Maxwell a beautiful woman and superb surgeon and Margaret Schultze a flamboyant woman but a wonderful teacher. He also brought with him Daniel Morton who had just finished a residency at Hopkins. He proved to be a favorite of a generation of trainees and fellow specialists.

Lynch was born in 1871. He received his A.B. at Western Reserve University in 1895 and his M.D. at Johns Hopkins in 1889. After postgraduate studies in Vienna and Munich (highly respected areas in our specialty), he was chosen as a member of the faculty at Hopkins until 1904. He was then on the faculty of Rush Medical College from 1909 to 1915 when he was offered the chairmanship at U.C.S.F. which he still held until 1942 when I met him. Shortly after a brief recovery, he retired and tried a light practice. Herbert Traut whom he respected replaced him. Lynch wanted to continue to look after his patients and set up an office in the city. Alice Maxwell thought she should have been given the office of chairman. And so did many of us. She had been the first woman to be chosen to be president of the most prestigious obstetrical and gynecological society in the country. She resigned and moved her practice across to Children's Hospital. When she retired, she left most of her practice to me.

When I returned from the war in 1945, Dr. Traut appointed me Assistant Resident. I was surprised one of my days in surgery to see that I was to help Doctor Lynch with the senior resident. Half way through the operation, Doctor Lynch backed from the table and told the chief resident to finish. Doctor Lynch commented on a number of things as he sat there. He died in his sleep not long after.

In his time as chief of the Department of Ob/Gyn at U.C.S.F., he did wonders. He established a superb training program. Most important is the fact that Doctor Lynch's house staff acted like a family. When Len Charvet, the chief resident decided to marry which was rare for residents to do, Doctor Lynch told him to use the department car to go to Yosemite, and he gave Len money to finance it all. There was a real effort to look out for each other during and after training. We had great respect for our faculty that Doctor Lynch had chosen. Doctor Maxwell was not only a great surgeon. She had a regal style. When she came to give a lecture to my class everyone stood as she came into the room. I scrubbed with her one day, and I said, "You do that just like Doctor Morton (our idol)." She replied, "It ought to be, I taught him."

Doctor Schultze was in charge of the service at the San Francisco Hospital. There was a big practice there because of severe pelvic infections. Those were from complications of venereal disease or abortion. She taught us how to deal with them before we had antibiotics and how to be supportive of the poor women who suffered. All of this was a reflection of Doctor Lynch's true concern for women. The team of Lynch, Maxwell, and Morton produced the best record of cure of cancer of the uterine cervix in the world. That included the radical operation for cancer of the cervix called, the Wertheim, which Doctor Lynch had learned in Austria and perfected before antibiotics or blood banks. We all became experts in vaginal surgery which general surgeons never learned well from my point of view.

Doctor Lynch received every honor a man in our specialty could receive in California and nationally. Included in these honors were the White House Conference on Prenatal and Material Care representing the American Board of Obstetrics and Gynecology. He was honored guest of the Pan American Surgical Congress. He wrote a book with Alice Maxwell on Pelvic Neoplasms, which became a standard text. His other publications were innumerable.

He was married in 1904 to Rowena Tying Higginson. Their son was Frank W. Lynch Jr.

"Doctor Lynch's dynamic force, untiring spirit, thirst for scientific research and his engaging and sympathetic personality, combine with his skill and experience as a surgeon, and his zeal advancing the interest of his students make him an exceptionally inspiring teacher. He had an earnest ease of expression that impressed his precepts in the memories of his students and which made him a leader in many scientific societies of which he was a member."

—Philip Arnot, M.D., George Ebright, M.D., Francis S. Smyth, M.D.

Doctor Lynch taught me to use marijuana to treat people dying from cancer. When heroin was made illegal, we were permitted to use what we had. Doctor Lynch bought a pound of it in time and we used it judiciously. His high-pitched voice continues to talk to me. My field was obstetrics and gynecology.

AFTERTHOUGHTS

When I returned home from World War II, I had been with combat infantry in Europe for about a year and a half, and I had accumulated a good number of points from battle stars, decorations, and time served. So, I was permitted to fly home on a beat-up plane that had flown into China. I had never been in a plane before. When I arrived home, I had loving greetings with my family. Surprisingly, I felt depressed. I did not want to go out. I spent time organizing photos I had taken. None of my male friends had yet returned and I tried dating some of the girls I had known and there was no spark. Finally, one day a friend of my parents said there was a girl I should meet. With some resistance I decided to take a chance. The girl's name was Gwen Miller. She lived in a lovely home in Saint Francis Wood, a residential area toward the edge of San Francisco. She was one of the most beautiful women I had ever met. She was a Phi Beta Kappa from Stanford, and she could dance like a dream. I decided almost at once that she was the girl for me. I know now why so many of our veterans cannot deal with their return home. There are not enough Gwens to go around.

When my children were grown, Gwen began volunteering in the medical staff office. She was soon asked to work as a part-time staff member particularly in the Cancer Registry. She has recently retired at the age of 91. They wanted her to stay. She is my personal hero. She got me out of my depressed state and keeps me there.

* * *

ABOUT THE AUTHOR

John A. Kerner, M.D., is a distinguished leader of the San Francisco medical community and former chief of obstetrics, gynecology and reproductive sciences at Mount Zion Medical Center, and a University of California San Francisco clinical professor of obstetrics and gynecology. Dr. Kerner was one of seven American WWII veterans awarded the French Legion of Honor by French president Nicolas Sarkozy at the home of the U.S. French ambassador in Washington D.C., November 2007. On 8 September of 2012, Dr. Kerner was inducted into the 35th Division's Hall of Fame which includes Harry S Truman and three Medal of Honor recipients. Dr. Kerner lives in San Francisco, California.

ACKNOWLEDGEMENTS

Though most of the contents of this book are memoirs, I found that at my age of 95, I needed help that I list below.

-J.A.K.

Season of the Witch by David Talbot portions related to Dianne Feinstein.

Cherokee Neurosurgeon by Brian Andrews concerning Charles Wilson, M.D.

The Charlton Story by Earle Perry Charlton II & George Winius, Chapter titled The Kapstein Window.

Many issues of the **San Francisco Chronicle** and its contributors concerning Herb Caen.

Combat Medic by John Kerner.

A Combat Medic Comes Home by John Kerner, concerning Herbert Traut, M.D., Alan Margolis, M.D., Mary Jane Brinton, Helen Rowan, and Governor Brown.

The New Yorker magazine Articles concerning Charles Wilson, M.D. and Dianne Feinstein. Especially, August 2, 1999.

The assistance of **David Newman** made the organization of this book possible.

John T. Colby Jr. of Brick Tower Press encouraged me to write this book. My thanks to him.

For sales, editorial information, subsidiary rights
information or a catalog, please write or
phone or email:

iBooks
Manhanset House
Dering Harbor, New York 11965-0342
Sales: 1-800-68-BRICK
Tel: 212-427-7139
www.ibooksinc.com
email: bricktower@aol.com

www.Ingram.com